THE MIND OF CHRIST

Anthony Duncan is an Anglican clergyman and author who lives in Hexham, Northumberland. He has written several classics of Christian spirituality, including *Pray and Live*, *Psychotherapy and Magic*, *Christ, Lord of the Dance* and *The Priesthood of Man*.

Other Christian titles published by Element Books

On the Prayer of Jesus
From the Ascetic Essays
Bishop Ignatius Brianchaninmov

Lost Christianity
A Journey of Rediscovery to the Centre of Christian Experience
Jacob Needleman

Theologia Germanica
Translated by *Susanna Winkworth*

Guided Meditation and the Teaching of Jesus
Joan Cooper

Heresy
Heretical Truth or Orthodox Error? A Study of Early Christian Heresies
Joan O'Grady

The Yoga of the Christ
In *The Gospel According to St John*
Ravi Ravindra

The Essene Odyssey
The Mystery of the True Teacher and the Essene Impact on the Shaping of Human Destiny
Hugh Schonfield

After the Cross
Hugh Schonfield

The Passover Plot
A New Interpretation of the Life and Death of Jesus
Hugh Schonfield

Those Incredible Christians
Hugh Schonfield

The Pentecost Revolution
Hugh Schonfield

Meister Eckhart Volumes I–III
Sermons and Treatises
Translated and edited by *M. O'C. Walshe*

THE MIND OF CHRIST

Meditations on Christian Themes

ANTHONY DUNCAN

Element Books

© Anthony Duncan 1990

First published in Great Britain in 1990 by
Element Books Limited
Longmead, Shaftesbury, Dorset

Cover photograph: Sixth century silver and gilt Byzantine
patan, courtesy of the Temple Gallery

Cover design by Nancy Lawrence

Designed by Nancy Lawrence

Text decorations by Jane Newton

Typeset by Footnote Graphics, Warminster, Wiltshire

Printed and bound in Great Britain
by Billings Ltd., Hylton Road, Worcester

British Library Cataloguing in Publication Data
Duncan, Anthony
The mind of Christ.
1. Christian life. Meditation
I. Title
248.34

ISBN 1–85230–185–6

Contents

Introduction

It is, perhaps, a matter of passing interest why a country parson should hide himself away in the shed at the bottom of his garden and try to write a book about God. When I set out to write a book about God. When I set out to write *The Mind Of Christ* I was only too aware of the wise words of Meister Eckhart ringing in my ears, 'Why does thou prate of God? Whatever thou sayest of him is untrue!'

There comes a time in every man's life – even a clergyman's life – when a great desire is felt to desist from words altogether and fall silent before **The Mystery**. It is during the years leading up to this time that one feels compelled to make a noise – to talk, to write – even to teach! Yet, these very activities are perhaps best undertaken when the initial enthusiasms have worn away and there is a certain resistance to the whole thing. A becoming diffidence is appropriate, to be overcome only by a sense of urgency and in a spirit of obedience. I dare to think that something like this compelled the author of this book to put pen to paper.

Every preacher knows the difference between having something to say and having to say something – and so does his congregation! And where books are concerned, particularly religious books, there is a difference between a budding author's great desire to write a book on a certain subject and having one's heart seized by a book which is absolutely determined to be written, even though the author has but the vaguest of notions, to begin with, as to what the subject matter might be. For good or ill, this book falls into the second category.

The Mind Of Christ is offered as a connected collection of meditations or provocations to meditation – things to think about and mull over in prayer. The structure of the book follows the pattern of that blessed aid to contemplation, the Holy Rosary. Now, for those who may not be familiar with this powerful tool, let me explain. The Rasary is organised in three sets of Mysteries upon which to dwell, each set being five in number. In just the same way, this book is organised in three sections, each of five chapters or sub-sections. The first section deals with fundamentals and the other two deal with the implications of these fundamentals, but on slightly different levels. Essentially, however, the book is for dipping into, and is not one to be devoured in a single sitting. At least its author doesn't think so! But once a book is in the hands of a reader, he or she may, indeed must, do with it whatever seems appropriate.

Although I am a Christian priest, this book is at some pains not to be institutionally 'Church'. The Christian Church is, in its essence, an organism – a living thing – transcending the boundaries of this life, death and the Hereafter. It is, however, of the nature of organisms that they organise, and the circumstances of this mortal life are such that organisations can quickly stifle, or at least obscure, their organisms. Christ is not to be contained within the four walls of a church building, however hard we sometimes try. Nor is he in the back trouser pocket of someone's hierarchy. We who believe, not in 'incarnations' but in **The Incarnation** have hardly begun to take the measure of the implications of our belief in two thousand years. Our Lord did not come to found a new, better world religion, but to liberate us from religion once and for all! Jesus Christ, God Incarnate, is far too big for religion! There is no Temple in the Heavenly Jerusalem; the Bible tells us that.

Some five years have passed since the writing of this book, and yet, about every word that is written I can say, in Luther's famous words, "here I stand, I can none other!". I hope that the book will communicate something of the Love of God in which its author abides and which contains, inherent within it, the driving desire to share with others. And so I can offer it to our Lord, and to His Holy Mother, in Love and in what I hope is the spirit of Obedience. And I can offer it to the reader too.

Anthony Duncan, 1990

PART ONE

The Inner Quest

The Kingdom of Heaven is within you. The time has come for external forms and expressions to be left behind. There is no Temple in the heavenly Jerusalem, for religion has no place in heaven.

Man is his own temple. A man's heart is the altar of God, for Christ Himself has a heart of flesh and blood the same as Everyman. Life flows outwards from the heart, and all returns to the heart. It is in a man's heart that God the Holy Spirit dwells and thus it is that Prayer is defined as 'standing before God with the mind in the heart'. The encounter is an interior one but there is nothing subjective about it.

The whole universe is contained within the human mind, for it abides within the Mind of God, and man is made in God's image. Thus the inner realities are more real than the outer. All things meet and find their proper place when the human mind is rooted in the human heart and there perpetually abides.

The task of man and woman both, with ever-mounting urgency, is to learn to abide with the mind in the heart for it is here that the Second Coming of Christ in Glory will first be made manifest. The whole of earth and all its creatures are contained within the human heart, and their transfiguration has already begun.

Love

Love can be described as disinterested concern for the total and eternal well-being of others. Love includes many related emotions. True love is self-sacrificial, even to death. Jesus Christ is the Incarnation of True Love.

Love is enthroned within the human heart. Thus the human heart is the ultimate Altar of God. A man, or a woman, must become centred and live from the heart. A life which is not heart-centred is not truly living and cannot abide.

It is possible for a man or woman to live at other levels altogether. They may be centred on the intellect; they may live by their emotions; they may live at a mainly psychic level or they may be dominated by their appetites. To live by any of these is, to some degree at least, a living death. Only by learning to abide in and from the heart will intellect, emotions, intuitions and appetites be transfigured and brought to their fulfilment.

Thus it is that love transcends all law and codes of conduct, for these regulate human wrong-centredness and preserve the peace which is no peace. A man or a woman must live with the mind in the heart. There, reason and intuition are brought into harmony and appetites and emotions begin to express true Love rather than the disorders of a wrongly-centred life.

The mind of a man or woman can choose where, within the total person, it will abide. Mind is impossible of definition because it is a mystery. The human mind is a mystery next only to the Ultimate Mystery, the Mind of God Himself.

Creatures exist in so far as they are thought by God. As all things in heaven and earth are creatures, none can comprehend the mind that thinks them. Mankind has a mind which is creative, but with a creaturely creativity. This creativity

4

comes to its fulfilment in a man or a woman when the mind abides in the heart.

The heart is the deepest depth and the highest height of a man or woman. There, at the heart, God the Holy Spirit dwells. The heart abides ever in eternity. The heart is timeless, and if a man or a woman would come to fulfilment, then the mind must abide at that point at which that which is called 'time' is contained within timelessness. From there, all thoughts of truth and peace proceed.

Contemplation is, in its essentials, the conscious abiding in peace with the mind at rest in the heart. It is the giving of the undivided attention of the will to God the Holy Spirit who dwells in the deep heart of every man and woman. This is the height and the depth of prayer. It is a learning of the habit of a loving and trusting repose which may abide regardless of the distractions and the activities of the outer world. It is in contemplation that the active life is released from the shackles of time and is enabled to be lived in the timelessness which is the context of the Divine Creativity.

The Heart

The heart of man is the centre of his being. In this he images his Creator, for the Heart of God is the unknowable essence of God from whence flow the energies of God by which God may be known by man.

The heart, therefore, is the Ultimate Mystery. The heart of man is, in its own creaturely way, man's own ultimate mystery, known only to God himself. Man's quest leads him in search of his own heart, for there he will find God. There also he will find himself, and there also he will find all other creatures.

All mystical experience is therefore man's encounter with

5

his own heart, for the heart is timeless and spaceless, transcending heaven and earth. All time and space is therefore contained within the human heart, and all creatures may be found therein. The energies of God and the energies of man are in complete union within the human heart, for man is made in the image and likeness of God.

There is but one creature, man. Every man and woman, past, present and to come, upon earth are persons of the One Being. In this mankind images the Triune God who creates him and sustains him in Being. There is therefore but one human heart, and it is the quest of every man and woman to find themselves in it, and to learn to abide with their individual minds and wills firmly emplanted within it.

It is within the depths of his own heart that a man or a woman will discover the universal heart of man, and as the Word was made Flesh and dwelt on earth among men, it is there also that they will encounter Christ, their Lord and their God.

The heart of man transcends every plane or dimension of being. All are accessible to a man or a woman whose mind abides, firmly fixed, in the heart.

The mind which abides in the heart becomes aware of whatever is appropriate when it is appropriate. Love alone is the criterion, there is no other. In love there is no idle curiosity. Love does not manipulate, neither does love exploit for its own ends. In love alone are all things accessible to a man or woman, and for such a one, whose mind dwells in the heart, all things abide in the Divine Compassion.

Compassion is the hallmark of the human heart. Compassion is the true relationship between persons, and man was created to have Compassion for the rest of creation. Man is a priest, and a priest is one who stands at the intersection of the worlds, or planes of being. He is the door through whom all commerce between the worlds takes place. Jesus Christ is the Great High Priest, and Christian men and women participate in His High Priesthood.

The work of Divine Grace in a man or a woman is slowly to transfigure the totality of that person. This in itself is the

6

activity of the Divine Compassion and it proceeds from the innermost depths of the human heart where God the Holy Spirit dwells. Transfiguration is the fulfilment of every man and woman. It is the revelation of the truth in them and of them, the fusion of their creaturely life with the eternal life which is the life of the heart of man as it abides in God.

Men and women cannot by any means imagine the fullness of their own being from within the limiting confines of earthly life. Indeed the very distinction between man and woman belongs to this earthly life, for as Jesus taught, in heaven they shall be as the angels, neither marrying nor being given in marriage, but complete.

It is only by learning to live with the mind in the heart that mortal man can escape being led astray, by unrooted and unconsecrated intuition upon the one hand, or by an arrogant and blinkered rationalism upon the other. The perfectly integrated man or woman abides in complete openness and balance because he or she abides in and from the heart. Integration is the great work of Divine Grace, and it requires from the human will its utter dedication in self-forgetting Love. This, too, is a work of Grace, enabling what nature seeks to intend.

The Divine Compassion is such that the work of integration proceeds almost in spite of human nature. But Christ has taken mankind's fallen and flawed nature to himself and transfigured the flaws into means of Grace. The vicissitudes of earthly life, the imbalances and the frequent lapses are turned into a 'School for the Service of the Lord', and all within the context of an ambience of forgiveness and everlasting Compassion.

Thus Paul asked, in perplexity, 'Shall we sin the more that Grace may abound?' It is a measure of the Divine Compassion that this often appears to be a genuine dilemma. It was the Prodigal Son in the parable whom Jesus portrays as the more attractive of the two!

The Quest

Man is one being, with an infinitude of persons. Men and women are thus participators in one another. The individual cannot be isolated, for he or she participates in everything that is happening, or has ever happened, in heaven or on earth.

Man is an eternal being and the persons of this being are likewise eternal, though it does not follow that every individual fulfils his or her immediate potential. The mystery of human life on earth alone is altogether beyond mortal man's comprehension. How much more so is the mystery of human life in its totality?

Communication between persons is dependent on love alone. Where there is no Love there can be no true communication at any level. Exploitation at any level is a falsehood by definition and belongs to that part of a man which is as yet unregenerate.

There are many counterfeits of which a mortal man or woman must beware, and counterfeits of love are the most deceiving of all. All true communication is between minds that are firmly rooted in the heart. For such, the boundaries of heaven and earth are no boundaries at all; the distinction has become unreal for heaven is present and operative within them all.

There are counterfeits, but they may be discerned by their character. The ability to discern is a grace, a gift of God, and transcends altogether the limited capacity to discern which belongs to the nature of every man or woman.

'Bear ye one another's burdens,' said Jesus. The obligations of love transcend the boundaries of time and space, of heaven and earth, of mortal life and that which is Wholly Other. This is a matter of the human heart, and those who would love one another must learn to abide forever therein.

8

The heart, that is to say the innermost depths of a human being, is the throne of God within him. Here the Holy Spirit dwells. Its abode is timelessness and, while unique and distinct in all creation, it is one with the universal heart of man. For a man or a woman to discover and to abide in this innermost depth is to have discovered the innermost truth of his or her own unique being.

By the same token, true self-discovery is allied to the discovery of God as he is knowable by the mind of man. And with this two-fold discovery comes the discovery of all other men and women, and of the totality of creation. This is the quest of everyman. It is the great work of grace within him, enabling and transfiguring the nature by which his own efforts must proceed.

This quest is not attained suddenly. It is a growing process, a slow penetration to the heart and a slow discovery of it. But the fruits of that discovery begin to be manifest as the quest is followed. The quest is endless because the heart of man is infinite and its depths can never be plumbed. A man may be given glimpses and foreknowledge of depths, or heights, beyond anything his unenlightened mind can conceive. He may begin to manifest graces (of which he himself is usually unaware) far in advance of the state of inner development at which he has arrived. He may advance on one front and be held up on another. There are many pitfalls and wrong turnings and not a few blind alleys on the way. But if he is faithful and steadfast, he will attain his quest, for God wills that he should.

The saddest of all men or women are those who have begun, and come far on their quest, and have then lost heart, lost faith in the forgiveness in which they abide, and have given up. It were almost better never to have started. It is never too late, however, to rise up and begin again.

The heart, the inmost being of a man, is where truth and reality abide. A man's quest is therefore an inward journey to the centre of his being. By no means, however, is this an introverted or self-regarding exercise. On the contrary. The more steadfastly a man looks *outwards*, away from himself, the better his progress within. Conversely, the more inwardly self-regarding he is, the more surely will he impede his inner growth.

The inner quest of a man or woman must therefore find its expression externally, in the ordinary things of everyday life. But it is necessary to be aware of the facts of human life, chief of which is that all worthwhile outward activity proceeds from inner motivation. It is the quality, the level of motivation which determines the nature of outward activity. The selfsame activities can proceed from very different motivations. In the world, men and women are judged by their outward acts. In truth, the judgement rests upon their inner motives. Heaven does not award orders or medals, neither is there a hierarchy as the world knows it. There is only one motivation known to heaven, and that is love.

So it is that love is the fulfilling of the law, as Scripture makes plain. Law has to do with outward observance; Love is concerned with inner motivation by which alone men and women are judged.

The God within is worshipped and discovered *without*. Only thus can men and women be rescued from worshipping their own ego as a god. In reality, the distinction between the 'without' and the 'within' is as temporary and contingent as that between time and timelessness. These are all temporary but necessary parameters without which mortal life on earth cannot be lived. They must be acknowledged, but not regarded as absolutes. The heart of man transcends and contains all these categories, as every man and woman shall, one day, discover.

Human life on earth is lived within the parameters of time and space. They present themselves as absolutes to the mortal man and woman. They are nothing of the kind, and an instinctive awareness of this drives men on to transcend them, to reach beyond them in the search, however perceived and expressed, for ultimate meaning and fulfilment.

This search must needs be an interior one and it may be

conducted in many ways and with many very different motivations. To explore within, however, is fraught with grave peril. Only the single-minded quest for the heart of man, the self-forgetting search and reach beyond self to God as he may be known and perceived by the mortal mind, will steer the searcher safely between the rocks and hidden reefs upon which he must otherwise be shipwrecked.

Only from within the depths of the heart of man are these apparent absolutes transcended, and from that viewpoint their worth, indeed their necessity, becomes plain. Man's life on any plane of being requires something corresponding to these two parameters if only in order to objectify the consciousness of a man and enable him to relate both to himself and to his fellows. Only in relation to God himself are these parameters finally transcended; yet they remain as it were ever-present to bestow a context upon a man in his everlasting quest into an eternally deepening joy and a forever unfolding fulfilment.

Forgiveness

Man is a sinner. Sin is a falling short and man, the being, is in the state of having fallen short. Having said this, there is little more to be said on the subject. What is important is that Christ has taken the 'fallen short' humanity to himself and it is this 'fallen short' humanity which, in him, sits at the right hand of the Father. There is a new beginning, a new creation, a whole new contract for human life and existence.

By the same token, the accidents and the calamities of human life are turned into means of Grace. Death itself is transformed, there is no ultimate defeat, no ultimate frustration, no ultimate despair. Everywhere and in everything there is hope and the possibility of joy and fulfilment. Christ is Risen. The context of mortal man is Eternal Life and he abides in an ambience of forgiveness and restoration which is forever his for the asking.

But it is before all other things necessary that both man and woman first of all acknowledge themselves to be sinners. Without a coming to terms with this central reality of human life there can be no forgiveness received, no work of grace can proceed, and eternal life cannot be participated in.

It is not a man's misdeeds which make him a sinner. It is not by keeping to a code of law that he is saved. All this is folly. A man is a sinner *by definition*. What can be expected of a sinner but acts of a sinful nature? There is nothing about a man or a woman that is not, in some way, 'fallen short'. This is the human experience and it is the human condition. A man must acknowledge this fully and freely; he must then get on with the business of living his life and growing by grace into the fullness of life eternal.

Perfection

Perfection is not a static concept, it is a dynamic process. To be perfect, as Jesus commands his followers, is to be in the Way of Perfection. This implies constant forward movement, perpetual development, the steady realisation of potential and the everlasting bestowal of new and greater potential.

An approach to the idea of perfection which is based solely upon pious exercises, asceticism and tightly defined codes of conduct is both static and stultifying. There is a place for pious observance, provided that it is the outward expression of love in the heart. There is a place for asceticism, provided that it is a healthy self-discipline undertaken for love's sake. There is a place for codes of conduct, provided that they are understood as general guide-lines for the immature, and that they truly reflect outgoing and self-forgetting Love and do not encourage neuroses or guilt-ridden fantasies.

Perfection is a dynamic way which is trodden by love for love's sake. It reflects the character, the personality, of the ever-blessed Trinity. Its keynote is self-forgetfulness. The Way of Perfection is full of apparent paradox; the Prodigal Son, in Jesus' parable, was on the Way of Perfection. His foolishness, his spendthrift behaviour, his dissolute living were, in a sense, consecrated by his final penitence. They led him to the discovery that he was a sinner with no righteousness of his own, deserving nothing but the trough of despair into which his own free will had led him. In his repentence, however, they are turned – transfigured – into a means of

13

grace. The very means of grace, indeed, that had put him into the Way of Perfection and restored him to his Father, no longer only a son, but now a beloved friend as well.

By contrast, the good boy, remaining obedient at home, had not yet begun. It would be his father's rebuke that would, for the first time, turn his feet into the Way of Perfection, which is otherwise described as the way of human maturity and true responsibility.

Sin

Sin proceeds from the heart. It is the heart of man that is corrupted, and all men partake of the corruption. But Christ has taken that corrupted heart to himself. The cost was the death of his humanity on the Cross. Not for nothing did the Roman soldier lunge for the heart when he pierced the dead Lord with his spear. Corrupted heart lunged at the heart of eternal Love, projecting its own self-hatred upon the other.

Mankind abides in an ambience of forgiveness and restoration. The death of humanity was manifested in Jesus. The new and eternal life is manifest in the Resurrection. Humanity is risen and ascended. The heart of man, still corrupted, is healed and man is re-created.

Individual men and women, partaking of the effects of corruption within them, have that very corruption available to them as a means of grace; for it is within the heart that God the Holy Spirit dwells. The All-Pure dwells within the impure, and even its impurity is turned into the Way of Perfection.

There is therefore no escape for any man or woman from the deviations and the impurities of the corrupted heart. Its imbalances will forever affect him, but as he grows towards maturity and learns compassion for himself as well as for other men, he will learn to put even the impurities to good account and to turn all manner of deviations to the best and most loving account.

For sin has been described as worship which has missed the mark. There is profound truth in this and its truth will be made ever plainer. A man will learn by God's Grace the subtle and the loving ways by which the mark may become ever clearer and the near-misses redirected to the place where they should be.

Repentance

To repent is to 'turn round'. The life of man on earth is therefore a perpetual struggle with his own steering gear which has become fouled.

A man's earthly pilgrimage is best likened to a sea voyage. He navigates by the stars, relating always to the Pole Star which is Christ. There are many storms and not a few uncharted reefs. He must frequently take soundings with great care, and he must often follow his inner guidance and take a chance of great risk.

But his steering gear is faulty and his motive power fluctuates. He must learn the most consummate seamanship as he sails on his voyage. The voyage is as long as it happens to be.

Repentance is a perpetual task. It begins with the recognition that the steering gear is faulty. No progress is possible until this is recognized. Thereafter the inner man must remain at the helm, night and day, feeling the vessel beneath him, sensing danger, applying the corrections that he learns as he goes, and not infrequently waiting for the tide to float him off a sandbank on to which, by inattention or neglect of duty, he has grounded.

A man must expect damage. Storm damage, damage near the water-line as his faulty gear brings him into collision with other vessels. Damage beneath the water-line as he strikes a rock. Sometimes a man limps home despite battle-damage enough to have sunk him. Seamanship of the highest order is demanded, and all watches must remain alert.

But his must be a happy ship. He must learn the secret of joy. This will be his surest compass and his most efficient damage control as well. He must steer with his mind in his heart if he is to arrive at the berth prepared in advance for him.

Asceticism

Asceticism is a tool to be used to aid the perpetual process of repentance. But asceticism must not become an end in itself or it will inflate the very ego its practice is intended to discipline and restrain.

Ascetic practice must be governed by sound common sense and must give expression to love. Asceticism must be an expression of respect for the very lower nature that is being brought under discipline and the appetites that are being subjected to Godly restraint. Its object is the fine tuning of the inner muscles; it is a 'keep fit' exercise which partakes of the nature of prayer.

The body is part of the human whole. It is the earthly expression of that unique set of proportions which is the essence of every man and woman as they are known by Almighty God. A human being is *expressed* on every plane of being, in heaven and on earth. The expression is appropriate to the context but it always reflects the archetypal set of proportions which is the unique essense of every person. Ascetic practice maintains the integrity of the expression because it is a discipline both of body and of mind.

16

Asceticism must not be earth-denying or disfiguring. Extremes are at all times suspect and a sign either of immaturity or of a pathological condition. A failure to bring the lower self under discipline however, is a failure in humanity. It is a pandering to corrupting comforts and the lesser good, and will swiftly enthrone appetite as a god.

Ascetic practice must be positive. It must seek to achieve a positive aim rather than seek to avoid this, that or the other excess. As soon as the principle of avoidance is allowed to predominate, the excesses to be avoided are turned into bogeys and all manner of anxieties are induced which defeat the whole object of asceticism. Common sense must govern the whole practice, allied to a true compassion for a mortal man or woman's flawed condition. The motive of the whole exercise is love.

Asceticism takes many different forms. Abstinence from food or drink, or from minor luxuries, is the most common. Fasts during Lent and Advent, and in some traditions before important days in the Church Calendar, have as their underlying intention an offering of the will, a purifying of the body and a general heightening of the awareness in preparation for the Truth which is to be celebrated at the conclusion of the fast. Fasts rely upon freely willed and ready cooperation between mind and body. A fast undertaken because it is a social or religious convention, and without conscious involvement and intention, is worthless.

Fasting is, however, only one form of asceticism. Another is the undertaking of a positive discipline rather than a negative. A task will be undertaken, a job will be done, a neglected talent will be fostered by daily practice. A discipline of recreation and relaxation is positively ascetic to one who is inclined to be obsessive about work.

Asceticism is a response to a need. It is one important way of applying necessary correction to the steering gear which will keep the vessel off the rocks and avoid grounding on shifting sandbanks. Any form of asceticism involves a more than usual motivation and the determination of the will to

17

embark upon it in the first place, and to persevere for the length of time determined upon.

Fasts are for a fixed period of time. There are a number of ascetic practices which can healthily become a normal feature of life – in which case they cease to be ascetic for that person – but for the most part it is important to set a limit and a definite termination to a period of asceticism. Failure to do so can induce an ego-centred pride in a person's ability to be an ascetic. It can also, in some cases, induce a pathological condition.

Common sense and good humour should be the hallmark of any form of ascetic practice. The absence of either is an indication that something is decidedly wrong.

Guilt

Guilt is the most damaging emotion that can afflict a man or a woman. Guilt is totally negative and has very little to do with repentance. Guilt is essentially an ego-centred emotion and it carries with it, on the one hand an implicit denial of forgiveness, and on the other hand, it assumes that all men and women are not sinners unless they have done something wrong. The guilt-ridden are frequently aghast at the thought that their own ego has been found wanting. The great 'me' has actually failed, and guilt becomes a wallowing in self-centred negative emotion.

Guilt is essentially inhibiting. It prevents objective assessment, it denies forgiveness because the ego is unwilling to forgive itself for being fallible. There is no compassion where guilt reigns supreme, and guilt projects itself upon others at the least opportunity.

Guilt is a powerful motivator, but its motives are morbid. Many men and women are driven by guilt, and many who are not driven by their own guilt are driven and tormented by the guilt projected upon them by their fellows. Guilt is the driving force behind perfectionism. The ego cannot endure to discover itself fallible and therefore it must conceal its vulnerability behind perfection in all things.

It is necessary that the ego learn to accept its fallen condition and to forgive itself within the context of the forgiveness in which it forever abides. Without self-forgiveness, the Divine Forgiveness can never have full effect because it cannot be received. A man must learn to acknowledge that he is a sinner by definition. He must learn to accept that his ego will be outraged by its own fallibility and he must learn to forgive himself, formally and consciously, and to renounce all guilt as a positive act of faith.

Absolution

Repentance involves more than the individual for we are all members one of another. Sinfulness is a shared condition and the outward manifestations of the inner disorder impinge upon mankind at large.

There is no misdeed too bad to find its echo in the heart of every man and every woman. There is no sin, no horror, no degradation that is not present in principle in every human heart. The potential is ever-present and it is of universal application and experience.

A man must therefore forgive himself. He must forgive his neighbour. He must seek forgiveness of his neighbour and he must know himself not only forgivable but objectively forgiven. This is the great gift to mankind of sacramental confession and absolution. It is the great gift to mankind of psychoanalysis and similar ministries of men and women to each other by which they know themselves and each other, and learn compassion and know forgiveness.

19

The memories of a man must be healed and forgiven. This ministry goes very deep for a mortal man's hurt memories are not merely his own. We are members one of another and we inherit memories which are in need of healing for the hurt contained within them inhibits us and casts shadows over our lives.

Facing memories can be very painful. Frequently a man needs the help of others in order to do so, but God the Holy Spirit is the best of all analysts and will reveal a person to himself, or to herself, directly from within or indirectly through the ministry of other men and women, and also through the Ministry of the Holy Angels.

Loving absolution is the most blessed of all ministries that a man or a woman can either perform or receive. The healing of the memories is an essential ingredient for spiritual wholeness and growth in grace.

True repentance is an activity of Divine Grace. Divine Grace assists and enables the endeavours of a mortal man's flawed nature. As a lifelong process, Divine Grace transforms and transfigures the whole of nature and repentance itself becomes a Divine activity within a man's heart.

The first work of Divine Grace is to reveal to a man, or to a woman, the truth concerning the self. Sometimes that revelation of self to self is sudden, dramatic and exceedingly traumatic. More often it is a more gradual process during which lapses and misdeeds are turned into means of Grace and a gradual growth to maturity is the result, with Compassion and an understanding of the lapses of others a feature of that maturity.

An attitude of mind which resembles a rulebook full of acts of sin which are to be avoided and strictly censured when they occur is profoundly immature and betrays an absence of compassion. Condemnation and scandal over the lapses of others is more often than not a form of projection of similar disorders within, unresolved and unrepented of. It indicates a denial of the reality of the ambience of forgiveness in which the whole of mankind abides, and a lack of awareness of the

20

character of the Father as revealed in the Incarnate Son. It is a manifestation of an absence of true faith.

The ultimate scandal is the Love of God for sinners. All men and women are sinners, not by deeds but by definition. This is the context – the only context – for the operation of Divine Grace. Jesus reminds us that there is more joy in heaven over one repentant sinner than over ninety-nine righteous persons in no need of repentance. Little wonder! There are no righteous persons at all, and those who imagine themselves righteous are in a state of spiritual death which is the antithesis of all joy.

Men and women are forgiven for the asking. Guilt feelings must be put away and forgiveness taken with the Love with which it is offered. But they must live with the wounds they have afflicted and received. These, accepted, will become means of Grace. All are sinners, none may pass judgements, none dare withhold forgiveness.

Forgiveness may be offered vicariously and received vicariously, for all are one in the one being, man, and all are in Christ. There is no circumstance whatever in which forgiveness is impossible. At worst its acceptance can be delayed and inhibited by an unwillingness to forgive another or one's own self.

Forgiveness transcends the boundaries of heaven and earth. The living may absolve the dead for all are alive, and only the unforgiving are dead.

The New Humanity

Mankind on earth is man and woman. Each is complete and at the same time each is made complete by the other; thus marriage is the way to wholeness for the great majority. In the giving of self to another in the completeness possible when matrimony is holy – enabled, that is, by Divine Grace – the union of Christ with His Bride the Church is both imaged and celebrated. Each can see God in the other and the other in God, and the total intimacy of shared lives can remove all fantasy. When matrimony is holy it is also real in a unique manifestation of reality.

Marriage is also a way of the Cross. Not for nothing are bride and bridegroom crowned in orthodox weddings. Those who are in Christ know no crown other than that of martyrdom. Martyrdom is far wider and subtler a process than simply being put to death for the faith. Most martyrdoms are lifelong and may involve illness, incapacity of self or a partner, betrayal, frustration, what the world calls failure, and terrible hurt and disappointments. Martyrdom is that which men and women, and their children, inflict upon each other. In extreme cases this involves violent and premature death, but that is only one facet of the jewel.

Martyrdom is thus a means of grace, for we are all members one of another. A hurt lovingly accepted is the profoundest prayer the hurt one can offer to those inflicting the pain. Within the context of marriage this is a commonplace, and by the action of Divine Grace both grow into an ever-deepening and mature union of such a character as to transcend the boundaries of heaven and earth, this mortal life and the fuller life which follows it and is to come.

Failure, however, is the common lot of mortal man and woman. All are sinners, and without the enabling ministry of Divine Grace nothing can be brought to its true fulfilment.

Polarity

The principle of polarity is of universal application. In mankind it is expressed very obviously in men and women. But in each man and each woman the principle finds expression; there is a masculine side to woman and a feminine side to man. These things are a commonplace.

The principle flows from the relationship between the Creator and creatures. It finds expression in the minds of men through such concepts as 'yin-yang' and the various esoteric philosophies of like nature which observe a fact of life but build much specious wisdom into complicated systems and doctrines. With these we are not now concerned.

Man is born of earth as his mother and the sky as his father. Such is the burden of his primitive religious instinct. He must leave the apron strings if he is to mature and at the same time engage in trials of strength with his father. What holds good for an individual holds good for the whole. The earth-mother becomes, for him, a dark and child-devouring power which he must escape. Mythology abounds with stories of this kind. But he must return, not as dependent child, but as Friend. The old 'goddess' must be rediscovered, but not as once she was.

The formal title, *Theotokos*, 'God-bearer' or Mother of God, bestowed upon Mary the Mother of Jesus, is a recognition that she is the human incarnation of the mother principle.

23

In her, the old earth-mother is transfigured. Her Son is not Adam, but the Second Adam. In him the whole of mankind is re-created. In him the universal mother is re-created in that she is deified in her Son. Not as goddess but as the Mother of God, and the human, created consort of the Father by whom the Word became Flesh and dwelt among us. In Mary, the Mother of God, man rediscovers the mother as friend. She is the fulfilment of his deepest psychological need, the transfiguration of his profoundest myths.

The Mother of God is more than a psychological necessity for man. She is flesh and blood. Her humanity ascended into heaven in and with her Son. Mankind is the summing up, the supreme expression of Earth and its life and so the mother-goddess has always been, in some sense, within Man and an integral part of him. Now this principle is fulfilled, transformed, externalised in strict objectivity. Mary is a human being, a woman, flesh and blood, deified by the Holy Spirit in her Son. She is what all mankind shall be because the Word became Flesh and dwelt among us.

Mary can never be separated from her Son. Each points to the other. The mystery of polarity is thereby perfectly expressed, yet in a way that utterly defies definition. It is of the nature of mystery that it defies definition, and this is one of the profoundest mysteries of all.

God can be known in and through the humanity of His Incarnate Son. Jesus is the human face of God by whom the Divine Personality may be personally encountered and known in human terms. Mankind can be known in and through the humanity deified of the Mother of God. God and man are wholly other, one the Creator, the other the creature. God cannot be known about in any sense, but He may be known through the Divine Humanity. Mary may be known, but the mystery of mankind is too deep for mortal man, a person of it, to comprehend.

A man's religious life is complete and in balance when the Holy Mother of God has a firm place within it. Without Mary, a man's Christian faith and life is in danger of distortion and disfiguration. The principle of polarity is too fundamental to be ignored. But Mary is not a goddess. She does not stand alone. Her place and function is always to point to her son, the Word who became Flesh. And he returns the complement by pointing to her, the archetype of all mankind, fulfilment of the Divine Polarity, and as formally defined by Holy Church: *Theotokos* or Mother of God.

The idea of polarity is profoundly biblical. The Divine Wisdom is seen as a feminine principle, consort and companion of the Creator. The mystical archetype of Israel, the *Shekhinah*, is also a consort in exile, awaiting the fulfilment. Israel is the wayward wife, the Bride. And the Song of Songs is interpreted as a song of love between Yahweh and Israel, His Bride; or later on as a song of Love between Christ and His Bride, the Church. The Church is the Body of Christ because first of all she is the Bride, and it is His body that the Bridegroom gives to His Bride.

Holy Scripture concludes with the vision of the heavenly nuptials, the marriage feast of the Lamb. Nuptial imagery and the principle of polarity are everywhere to be found.

Jesus is the expected Bridegroom. He identifies with this role and fulfils it as a matter of course. His teaching is full of nuptial imagery and the Last Supper contained all the essential features of a marriage feast.

Christ is risen, ascended and glorified. From the moment of the resurrection all things are changed. Mary, the Mother of God, is the embodiment of the *Shekhinah*, the mystical archetype of Israel. She is also the Church and Mother of the New Humanity.

The more deeply a man or a woman penetrate to and abide in the heart, the closer will be their contact with, and personal knowledge of the Holy Mother of God, and the profounder her influence upon them for their wholeness and the fulfilment of their humanity.

Mary points forever to Jesus. Jesus points to Mary. The two are inseparable but in no sense are they to be confused or identified. Mary is the Mother of her Lord and her God.

25

There can be no blurring of the distinction between Creator and creature, even though the creature is deified by the fulfilled activity of Divine Grace.

Husband and wife are together both an image and an expression of the polarity between the Creator and the creature. But let them beware of drawing conclusions from this which are distorted by social conventions and expectations concerning the relationship between men and women. Such an oversimplistic identification of maleness with Creator and femaleness with creature is a parody of the truth. There are male and female principles in both men and women. The difference between them in this world is far less significant than most people suppose.

A man sees God in and through his wife. A woman sees God in and through her husband. Each is transfigured in the other's vision, and all are sinners. Polarity has to do with creative force and constraining form; the first is a male attribute, the second a female. Without the two in equilibrium there can be no creation. Without both within a man and within a woman there can be no life. The external accidents of sex are of transitory importance anyway. In heaven they are neither married nor given in marriage, but like the angels. So Jesus reminds us. They are not thereby diminished but complete.

The lifelong union of man and woman is an icon of the relationship between Christ and His Church, between Creator and creature. The Mystery is expressed in the icon. An icon is of itself but wood and paint, flesh and blood. The part of man and woman is to worship and adore God in and through this Mystery in which they abide. They are a Sacramental Presence, each to the other, and the profoundest means of Grace, if only the Divine Grace can operate within their relationship and within the heart of each. But all are sinners and inclined to inhibit the work of grace, and so the fullness of their potential joy is but seldom realised in this mortal life.

Creating force and constraining form are the human

concepts which express an awareness of the dynamics of Divine Love in creation. These concepts find expression in many ways and according to several esoteric philosophies upon which altogether too much tends to be built. It is sufficient that this twofold dynamic be recognized, but as it is a Mystery it quite defies human definition.

Mary

Mary, the Holy Mother of God, was the constraint which gave form to the lifegiving Word. Jesus was born into the world. The constraining principle was first made manifest by the message of the angel of God to Mary. She could have refused her vocation. Constraint, which is manifest in woman, could have been exercised to excess and frustrated the Divine Will. But she knew herself to be the handmaid of the Lord and the perfect equilibrium of force and form was arrived at. The Word became Flesh and dwelt among us.

Mary, the Holy Mother of God, is human first and woman second; but in her, womanhood is deified. She is what all the shadowy goddesses and archetypes of man's infancy could never be; she is the consort of her Divine Son. Each points to the other; the begotten of the Father, the uncreated, points to the creature who bestowed human form upon Him in the constraints of the creaturely condition. And she points to Him, who is her Lord and her God.

A man and a woman, both creatures, equal in all respects and the perfect complement and fulfilment, either of other, image and express the selfsame dynamic of Divine Love in creation. Their love proceeds from beyond themselves and flows through them to beyond themselves, making them both expressions of and vehicles of Everlasting Love.

Mary, the Holy Mother of God, is encountered in and

through the heart of a man or woman. She is intercessor, guide, friend and Mother of all Christian people, and through them of all mankind. She is active in the process of the *becoming* of mankind, and through mankind, the whole universe.

Mary partakes in full measure of the Mind of Christ. Into this Mind must all mankind grow; for a human being, as he or she grows to maturity by Grace, begins to participate in this Mind. To participate in the Mind of Christ is to will and act in character with that Mind. Freedom within the Mind of Christ is absolute and all are free to initiate, for nothing initiated from within that Mind is out of character with Christ our God.

Mary, partaking of this Mind in fullest maturity and in her total fulfilment, initiates actively and effectively among mortal men and women. Always she points to her Divine Son. Mary is the first and foremost evangelist and her evangelism transcends the boundaries of heavenly and earthly being.

The dual dynamic of polarity is therefore resolved in her who is the deification of womanhood. She initiates and gives form to that which she initiates. In her, created beings may see the end to which they all aspire. Yet there is no end, for the Mind of Christ is eternal and ever-developing of its thoughts and intentions, with an infinite participation by those who have entered into it and manifest its character in their lives and being.

Christ

The Mind of Christ transcends the boundaries of heavenly and earthly life. It is the Mind which abides in the heart of Man, waiting only to be found and participated in.

The character of the Mind of Christ shows in all who

begin, however tentatively and uncertainly, to participate. It is the work of Grace to bring men and women to this Mind, for here the Eternal Life given to mankind begins to be truly lived.

It is participation in the Mind of Christ which brings a man or woman into a permanent abiding in the heart and it is in this abiding in the heart that causes all barriers, separations and unreal limitations to fade away. Those who participate in the Mind of Christ and abide in the heart are at one with, and in intimate communion with, the whole Communion of Saints and are in close fellowship with the Holy Angels of God.

The Holy Angels are not to be comprehended by mortal man. He may become aware of their presence but they are not of His order of being. They are, however, His closest and most devoted friends and guides, for they fulfil the Divine Will and are, according to their own order, the living embodiment of the Divine Will.

All the fellowship of heaven and earth is fully and freely available to one who participates in the Mind of Christ and whose character is conformed to that of Christ by the operation of Divine Grace. The exercise of that fellowship, the living of the life of the Communion of Saints, is the joy into which a committed and transfigured Christian is called. The desire of every Christian in this mortal life is to be transfigured by Grace and wholly possessed by the Holy Spirit.

Jesus the Christ is the Second Adam. This is a poetical description of the significance of His birth and ministry in the world, His death, resurrection and glorious ascension. There are no words adequate to articulate the Mystery of the Incarnation. Mankind is, as it were, given a new contract for existence. It is a re-creation in principle, that principle to be realised in the lives of individual men and women, but also in mankind as a whole. This process transcends the bounds of life on earth which is but a part of the whole.

Jesus the Christ, Son of the Living God; invites and draws

men and women into His Mind. They are invited to become like Himself, their characters transformed into conformity with His own, and their own unique personalities fulfilled within the context of the freely shared Mind.

Mary, the Holy Mother of God, is in this respect the forerunner for the rest of mankind. She has taken with her the earth-mother principle of man's infancy and fulfilled it. And in the Womanhood deified she has brought into complete equilibrium the twofold dynamic, force and form, male and female, while remaining in all respects Woman.

A man and a woman together minister to each other at every level by Divine Grace, and each helps the other towards the same fulfilment. Holy Matrimony depends upon the Divine Grace for its holiness, but in the context of a truly Holy Matrimony, the possibilities of men and women becoming what they are are immeasurably enhanced.

The Communion of Saints

The Communion of Saints is that fellowship of men and women who participate in the Mind of Christ and who abide in the heart. Their fellowship transcends all boundaries between worlds for they are the New Humanity, the brothers and sisters by adoption of the Second Adam. They abide in Christ and He in them. Their corporate life and being is the context of the operation of God the Holy Spirit within mankind.

Participation in the Communion of Saints is the inheritance of every Christian, and the growth in Grace during his or her mortal life is a growth into ever fuller participation in and experience of this all transcending and all loving fellowship. All are brothers and sisters, from the Holy Mother of God to the newest convert to Christ. All are united in love and available to each other for love's sake. Mortal men and women have to grow into this fellowship and learn self-abnegation, and come to partake of the character of Christ before the riches of this fellowship can be even glimpsed.

Each member of the Communion of Saints points to Jesus. He is their humanity, their character and their integrity. In His humanity, their humanity is deified, and through deified humanity the earth becomes the New Earth and one with the New Heaven.

Prayer

Prayer is a dialogue between two wills; the Will of God and the will of man. However the manner of conducting the dialogue may vary between persons and circumstances, and whatever may be the apparatus of prayer, the reality of it, at the deepest level, is this dialogue of wills.

The purpose of the dialogue is twofold. First, that the creature may come to know and to relate to its Creator in the personal terms which alone enable fulfilment to take place. Second, that the created will, by the self-imposed disciplines of prayer, aided by grace, may learn the habit of conformity with the Will of God, and enter fully into the Mind of Christ.

The apparatus of praying, its methods and techniques, valuable in themselves, are therefore strictly secondary. Even the words used are secondary as the true dialogue takes place at a level too deep and too exalted for words. The true articulation of the dialogue is conducted, in a Pauline phrase, in 'words which may not be uttered'.

The disciplines of prayer are therefore of the greatest importance. The verbal content, where words are used, is also important in that it must reflect a right doctrine if it is not to subtly distort and inhibit the dialogue. The prayers of silence are closest, in terms of human consciousness, to the inner reality but aids to recollection and meditation such as the Rosary are by no means to be despised. The totality of man must be engaged and posture, gesture or the dance can all play their part in promoting and maintaining the discipline of the will in giving its undivided attention to the Will of its Lord and its God.

The giving of the undivided attention of the will is the fundamental activity of prayer, and as it is done by a man's free will, aided by grace, it releases the Holy Spirit to operate upon and transform the creature from within.

The corporate prayer of the Church, whatever its form, be it the Divine Office or the Eucharist, is a giving of the corporate attention of the will to the Will of God. One form alone is of Divine institution and command. The Eucharist is offered in obedience to that command. It is in the offering of the Holy Eucharist that the Church becomes what she is.

The Eucharist

The Eucharist is the activity of Christ within re-created humanity. It is both the expression and the activity of the Heart of God and Man in perfect union. Its offering is a Mystery beyond all human knowing, yet the simplicity of the act is full of meaning and Grace at every level. The bread and the wine are symbols of man's being and function. He is steward over that part of creation of which He is a part and which provides the context of His being. The bread and the wine are the raw materials of nature transformed by the creative stewardship of Man. In bringing and placing them on the altar men and women bring both themselves and the rest of creation which is to be transfigured with them and through them. The Eucharist is an act of transfiguration and deification. God alone acts and the elements are taken up into the Ultimate Mystery to be returned and given and received as the Body and Blood of Christ. It is altogether impossible to comprehend or to define this Mystery. It is given by God and by it we receive God. The Mystery can be encountered and known in the depths of the being. It can never be known about.

The Eucharist is the invocation of the Totality of Christ. It is the invocation of transfiguration for mankind, and of the deification of mankind and of the fulfilment and glorification of all things through mankind in Christ.

The relationship of the Church to her Lord has been likened to that of Bride to Bridegroom. This imagery is deeply scriptural and it was enacted and fulfilled by the Lord himself as a matter of course during his earthly ministry. There is no human language so appropriate as that of the love of man and woman for each other to express the person to person love between God and Man, or Christ and His Church.

The Eucharist, therefore, is a profoundly nuptial celebration. It is the Marriage Feast of the Lamb as manifested on earth. It is the timeless reality made manifest in time. The Lord presides at His nuptials. He is the Bridegroom and His Church is the Bride. They celebrate their marriage and proceed towards the consummation of all things. The Eucharist is an invocation of the consummation of all things.

As for all, so for one. The Christian man or woman in prayer is the bride. The Lord is the Bridegroom, and both are beloved of each other. The end in view for the bride is the consummation of her union with the beloved, and the poetry of the mystical saints is full of this expectation and the earthly manifestation of its fulfilment is the Unitive Life.*

The Eucharist, therefore, is the summing up of the prayer of all who participate; and all who participate become the Bride by virtue of their participation. The prayer of the Church gives life to the prayer of the individual. It is not possible to isolate the one from the many or the many from the one. A Christian's altar is his or her own heart. It is there

---

* In the classical understanding, the Unitive Way, or *Via Unitiva* is the third and last stage of the spiritual life. After purgation in the Purgative Way, and illumination in the Illuminative Way, the soul enters on the Way of Union with God.

that the Lord celebrates His mysteries of Love. The Eucharist is celebrated on the altar which is the heart of the Church, both in heaven and on earth.

Prayer

Prayer is an activity which is both outgoing and interior at the same time. It is a dialogue of wills between persons, therefore, although in the profoundest sense the dialogue is conducted *within*, yet in the context of earthly life it must be externalised. Thus the Other is related to as if He were *outside* the being of the man or woman praying. In reality each is within the other, but the realities are beyond the possibility of adequate representation to the imagination of mortal man or woman.

The prayer is offered to One who is both Wholly Other and, in some sense, over against the person praying. It is necessary for the dialogue to be conducted from the human side as if it were a dialogue between two human beings in mortal life. However, just as the *rapport* between lifelong friends or a man and his wife may come to permit of a semblance of mutual indwelling, so prayer becomes gradually more and more interiorised as the man or woman enters more deeply into the Mind of Christ.

Sacraments express the human condition with great simplicity and profundity, for a sacrament has an outward and visible sign, exterior to the human person but relating to the earthly circumstances which are his or her context. The outward and visible sign is understood as conveying to the inner being the inward and spiritual Grace. Thus the 'outer and other' and the 'inner and other' are at one. This mystery is part of the Ultimate Mystery and therefore cannot be defined any more than the relationship of the human being to

35

the Creator can be adequately defined. Images and models are the best that can be hoped for in order that the understanding can grasp the essentials of the mystery and thus pass on from being understanding to becoming wisdom.

Prayer is a corporate activity. The one and the many cannot be separated and the prayer of the individual is a part of the prayer of Man as a being. For this reason, other persons impinge upon an individual's prayer and he or she finds that it is impossible to be 'alone with God'.

As a man enters more deeply into his heart and participates more fully in the Mind of Christ, so his awareness of the Communion of Saints will heighten and he will come to realise that the bounds of earthly life are transcended in prayer. Prayer is addressed to God, but others become involved in the process. This discovery is something that is *given*. It must not be sought, for there is a counterfeit at a lower, psychic level which may be encountered by those sensitive to these levels, but which is of nature only and not of Divine Grace.

The awareness of the Communion of Saints, and sometimes of the fellowship of the Holy Angels, is a gift of Divine Grace and one to be accepted gratefully but never misused. This awareness has no relevance of itself. It is a consequence of an awakening by Grace to realities not normally perceived, and its whole context is prayer to Almighty God.

Friends and brethren are friends and brethren regardless of their present mode of existence. The Communion of Saints transcends the bounds of mortal life and the man or woman praying, who encounters its wider reality, is in fact already a part of that Communion. The saints are those whose saintliness is wholly that of Christ. There is none other. Growth in Divine Grace is the exercise of the life of the Communion of Saints and the way into the fullness of its everlasting fellowship in Christ.

Prayer is active participation in the Mind of Christ. It is an activity of Love and it is conducted in a context in which it is impossible to be alone, yet possible always to be totally intimate.

Humility has been described as truthfulness; a truthfulness before God. It is the acknowledgement of reality. Reality includes sinfulness. It is before all things necessary that a man or a woman come fully to terms with the built-in fact of sinfulness. Total fallibility, once accepted, is total liberation, for Divine Grace alone can be relied upon and no false criteria are admitted. A mortal man or woman must learn to abide in the Divine Love which is the context of all being, and to rely absolutely upon the Divine Grace which alone makes all things possible.

Prayer, and the disciplines of prayer, are the way by which this is attained. Confession of sins is vital. Self-examination is vital. The Divine Grace will reveal all to the penitent who must learn to forgive self, for refusal to forgive self is the deadly sin of pride. The ego cannot come to terms with its total fallibility and therefore cannot forgive or receive forgiveness. This deadly pride must be broken. A man must love himself in truth before he can love his neighbour, and before he can truly return the Love of God.

Prayer is a process by which a man or woman is made whole and kept entire. During the process there will be many deaths and resurrections upon many levels. But we die in order that we may live. The process has dark and terrible periods which can last, sometimes, for many years. But these times are all manifestations of the Divine Love which purifies with fire. They must be endured, for suffering is the expression of love, and their endurance is the returning of the Divine Love to the Divine Lover.

The end product of prayer is that the man or woman praying shall become prayer incarnate. The activity of prayer, by the aid of the Divine Grace, must be transformed into a permanent state or condition. The very being of the man or woman must be perpetual prayer so that the Divine Grace may flow through them and from them in loving service to the totality of mankind, and to creation as a whole.

This is what it is to be an *Alter Christus*, the particular calling of all who are in Christ. By grace they must be adoration incarnate. By Grace they must be thanksgiving incarnate. By grace they must be penitence incarnate, and thus vicariously penitent for all men. By grace also their whole being must be transformed into intercession, and the Divine Compassion must be their motive force.

All this is totally beyond every possibility in terms of Man's unaided nature. But all things are possible for God, and all this is supremely possible in Christ. The process of becoming, however, is lifelong and requires total dedication. The dedication, however, is a dedication to self-giving Love of God in and through Jesus Christ, the Incarnate Son of God. No man or woman can do more than this, and this is also enabled by Divine Grace, or even this would be impossible.

Every Christian man and woman is to be an *Alter Christus*. There is no other meaning in their existence. The process of becoming is their whole life, and it embraces and transfigures the whole of life. It transcends the boundaries of this mortal life and it is, needless to say, a corporate undertaking, with the many within the Communion of Saints assisting and enabling the one through the overflowing from them of the Divine Grace in their Divine Compassion.

Prayer is the most normal, and should be the most natural activity for the entire human race. But Man is a sinner, and the created will of Man is flawed by what theology calls Original Sin. Therefore the will naturally falls short and is always inclined to choose a lesser good. The effort of giving undivided attention to the will of God is extreme. Without the assistance of Divine Grace it is virtually impossible. Divine Grace is able to act when the created will stirs of its own volition in a God-ward direction. Without such a stirring, Grace would be an intruder and this can never be.

Prayer, therefore, is beset by great difficulties which are only slowly and painfully overcome. The learning of the habit of conformity with the Divine Will is patchy, partial in any event, but slowly and inexorably cumulative providing the intent is maintained. Thus there is often more effort involved in beginning to pray at any time than in the praying when it is begun. And the torment of distractions can become almost intolerable. But the problems are never insuperable; Divine Grace is always sufficient if only it is given the slightest opportunity to act.

There is often great darkness to be endured by those who seek to pray in real earnest. The darkness is in part within themselves and springs from the battles fought deep within. In part also the darkness is no darkness at all but an excess of light so great that it is experienced as darkness by those to whom the light cannot be revealed at their present stage of growth.

To have seen the Uncreated Light is to have died and been born all over again in re-creation. The end in view is that all mankind shall be radiant with the Uncreated Light within shining through to transfigure the totality of creation.

Prayer is a process of emptying out. The whole apparatus of human presuppositions, projections and concepts has to be painstakingly cleared out and away, for God is Wholly Other and until all the man-made images and idols are removed, the reality cannot be encountered.

Yet it is the reality who is the removal agent. By Divine Grace alone man is able to clear away his concepts and presuppositions. Prayer is a process of falling silent, first here then there, throughout the entire depths of a man's being. It is a lifelong process at best. As each dark and cluttered corner is cleared out and the doors opened to the Holy Spirit, so other dark and cluttered corners are revealed. The sometimes disturbing inconsistencies of behaviour and attitudes of many of whom their contemporaries say that they are 'saintly' is evidence of this. Perfection is a way rather than a state, and any man or woman's entry into the Mind of Christ in this mortal life can only be partial.

The most fruitful approach to prayer with the intent to seek the inner silence is a concentration upon what God is not. Whatever the mind of man can conceive is not God. Every image is not God. There must be a total emptying of images and concepts before the being of man can be filled

39

with that which is beyond all images and concepts. This alone is the Lover of Mankind.

Emptying out is done in order to make room. A total clearance is necessary before there can be a total indwelling. Every concept, every image retained prevents the totality from being realised and it is the totality of the Divine Indwelling which is the end in view. Prayer is concerned with transfiguration, with deification. It is a two way operation and man's part in it is one of response to an Everlasting Love which would exalt him to a dignity altogether beyond the remotest possibility of his comprehension.

The many ways of praying are all articulations of the prayer which is conducted in the depths of a man's being. The whole apparatus of prayer enables the total person to be involved and provides something tangible for the discipline of the will to get to grips with.

A man will need many changes in his approach to the business of praying as life unfolds. His needs will change and the methods he employs will change with them. A harsh discipline at one stage will give place to a more relaxed discipline at another. The saying of verbal prayers will give place to forms of silent prayer. Meditation will give place to contemplation. Slowly, a relaxed and easy naturalness will emerge, together with an inner *rapport* which will make the Pauline injunction, 'Pray without ceasing,' more comprehensible.

To pray without ceasing, a man or a woman must *become* prayer incarnate. This is the first stage in their fulfilment. The process of fulfilment goes on through all eternity.

The Second Coming

The Coming Again of Christ in Glory is the ultimate hope of the Church on earth, and all manner of speculation has attended it. The images of Holy Scripture are poetic; there is a confusion between the ultimate and the immediate and, while praying for her Lord to come again, the Church has never been altogether clear what she is expecting.

This is inevitable, for the Mystery can only be hinted at. Calculations as to when this ultimate event might take place in history are all of them charged with unreality and foolishness. Nevertheless, the Mystery will be fulfilled but the categories of its fulfilment are not those which excite the imagination of mortal man, for his mortal, finite imagination is unable to rise to such heights.

The Lord, in his Second Coming, will complete a process begun at the Incarnation. This process is timeless and spaceless. It is beginningless and endless. Mortal man is obliged to relate the experiences of life on earth to time and space. His experiences have beginnings and ends. To speak, therefore, of timeless and spaceless realities, beginningless and endless, is to go beyond the capacity mortal man possesses for comprehension.

Nevertheless, these unfamiliar categories must be maintained, though they cannot be completely grasped, if grasped at all. The heart of Man, wherein God the Holy Spirit dwells, which abides in timelessness and in which time-ridden men and women must learn to abide, is the point at which the

Ultimate Mystery of the Second Coming will begin to be perceived. Once perceived, the Mystery will be revealed, but until this is the case the Church must continue to pray with the writer of Revelations: 'Amen. Even so; come, Lord Jesus!'

The Second Coming will impinge upon history, just as the Incarnation was an historical event. In both cases the timeless manifests in time. Time, however, is but a device for measuring duration as mortal man experiences it. It has no ultimate necessity or reality.

The manifestation of the timeless in time is essentially an interiorly perceived reality as far as mortal man is concerned. That which is interior becomes exteriorised. The process does not work in the opposite direction in the first instance. The interiorisation of that which is exterior is another matter altogether, and secondary.

The common error of the man in the street is to suppose that the exterior is the real. This is altogether mistaken. The real is the interior. The exterior is but a manifestation of the real in the context of time and space, neither of which are of ultimate reality. The inner life of man is therefore his true life. This is the Life which is Eternal and it is the context of his encounter with his God. In human relationships the inner realities of persons establish *rapport*. A relationship based upon exteriors only is sub-human and unworthy of animal creation.

Mortal man must therefore learn to look within and to regard with a new respect what is encountered there. The insights of psychology enable much that is morbid or merely subjective to be recognized for what it is. Introversion is a morbid condition. Introspection is a healthy activity. Prayer is essentially an interior activity, dealing with interior realities and relationships of a truly interior nature.

It is from within that the Second Coming will be first perceived. Let a man be wakeful. Let him learn to abide with his mind in his heart.

The true dwellingplace of man is in timelessness. In earthly life he has a dual responsibility; first is his stewardship of the earth and its creatures. Second is his maintenance of his inner integrity upon which in any event faithful stewardship depends.

The maintenance of man's inner integrity is the work of his will, enabled by Divine Grace. The stewardship of the earth and its creatures is a work of loving fulfilment, a priesthood to creatures which can only proceed from and be motivated by the Divine Love in which man is called to participate in full and creative consciousness.

The enormity of man's fall and continuing failure is manifest in his self-indulgent rape of the earth and its creatures. It is a betrayal of love, a denial of all integrity and is motivated by a self-destructive, self-hating despair. Man has long been slave to forces of evil beyond himself. He is slave no longer unless he chooses so to be. In Christ he is altogether a free man who has to realise by Divine Grace the freedom that is his. The consequences of his misdeeds, however, are inescapable in that plane of being upon which they are committed. Nothing is lost to God, but much may be lost for mankind. In Christ alone is man able to become himself and to realise and fulfil his God-given stewardship and priesthood.

The account that every man and woman must give of their own exercise of stewardship and priesthood is given in the timelessness in which their innermost being resides. It is from this timelessness that the consequences come and are manifested in man's earthly context of time and space.

The Second Coming cannot be predicted in terms of time and space, or in terms of historical process. It comes from beyond all such categories and therefore mortal man wastes his time, dissipates his energies and muddles his mind in attempting meaningless calculations and predictions. Similarly, the style and form of what is best described as 'the age beyond the End' is beyond man's imagining. It is sufficient that, knowing neither the day nor the hour, mankind should watch and be alert.

This watching and this alertness is an interior activity. As such, it manifests itself in exterior terms but these are not

43

important of themselves. Much watching and most of the alertness is vicarious. Mankind is one; men and women are members one of another and therefore the watching of the few is performed on behalf of the many. It is mankind as a whole which will come under judgement at the Second Coming. Individual men and women will partake of that judgement, but it is good to remember Abraham before the destruction of Sodom. A very few faithful can save a very great many by their faith and by their participation in the ever-loving and all-forgiving Mind of Christ.

The first duty of the Church is to herald the Coming of Christ in Glory. It is curious that any duty other than this seems to be preferable, even to the extent of casting learned doubts upon any Second Coming at all! However, that which is inexorable is inexorable. Its timing is in timelessness and its first encounters will be met within the innermost depths of the human heart. It were better for men and women that they be prepared.

The Eucharistic worship of the Church is an invocation of the Second Coming. It celebrates the Incarnation, the death, Resurrection and Ascension of Christ and it looks forward to His Coming Again in Glory. The Eucharistic memorial, *anamnesis*, is best understood as an invocation of the Saving Mysteries of Christ in their totality. This totality includes the Second Coming.

This invocation of the Saving Mysteries in their totality is what lies behind the Dominical injunction, 'Do this in remembrance (invocation) of me'. Jesus Christ did not come to found a new and better religion. He was and is the fulfilment of all religion. He was not concerned with liturgy as such or with innovations in worship. He came for the express purpose of restoring human integrity, of raising humanity to a new and 'other' level of being and of effecting in humanity as a whole what He was and is in Himself: the perfect human expression of God; the perfect union of Godhead and manhood. To this end, the invocation of the fulfilment of the Mystery is to be understood as being on a

44

wholly other level than liturgy as such, para-liturgy and the pieties of religion, admirable though they may be.

The Church exists on earth to proclaim the Kingdom and to invoke its consummation. This she does by being what she is, the Bride of Christ and His Body. She becomes what she is at the altar when, in obedience, she invokes the Saving Mysteries in their totality. All else flows from this.

Just as no individual can become himself except by the operation of Divine Grace within, neither can the Church become herself without the same. The one and the many may accept or refuse the Divine Grace; the choice is at all times their own.

Death

Death, to mortal man, remains a terror and a dark and seemingly impenetrable mystery. The Second Coming is identified by many with an idea of the end of the world which is terrible and full of death in its most dreadful aspect. This is wholly in error. The Second Coming is indeed the end of the world, but the 'world' as the Fourth Gospel presents it; the armed truce masquerading as peace, the whole apparatus of false criteria, injustice, cruelty and horror that men call civilisation. That will pass away and it will die from within.

Death is the great hope of mortal man, did he but believe, for it is the inevitable end of life on earth and the beginning of New Life. And all within the context of beginninglessness and endlessness. Death, the awful terror and the ultimate despair of man, is no more. The sting is drawn, the grave is deprived of its victory. There is a sense in which death is no longer of importance, for Life transcends it absolutely and it is but a stage upon a road.

The end of the world of false criteria and compromised

integrity will involve a great deal of dying and will seem, to those committed to worldly criteria, to be the ultimate despair. But it is nothing of the kind. To those participating in the Mind of Christ it will be quite other.

The Second Coming will be perceived from within. There will be either a dying from within, or a fullness of Life from within flooding through the totality of a man's or a woman's being. Whatever the outward vicissitudes may be, nothing will be lost and all will be gained. Death will be swallowed up in victory.

The Great Return

There will be an end, so far as man is concerned, to all that is evil which invades him from beyond himself. This, at the Second Coming, will complete a process which mortal man can only partially comprehend, and then in terms of poetic images and myth.

Comprehension is one thing, experience is another; and man has had a full burden of experience of that to which he has been in thrall but to which he need be in thrall no longer. It is not good for men and women to dwell upon these dolours or to speculate about them. It is sufficient that the 'prince of this world' – the author of false criteria, the father of lies and the ultimate hater of self – is cast out. The rest may be left to God.

The evil in man is, in part, his own. This may be utterly transmuted by Love and turned, through repentance and suffering, to means of great grace. There is no end to the possibilities of penitence and no end to the Love of God for sinners. Free will, that which makes man fully human, bears within it the possibilities of evil and must ever do so. The evil of human false choice, uncomplicated by evil which is 'other'

46

and which is always seeking to snare men and women and establish a foothold, is containable in charity, transmutable in love and evocative of the compassion both of God and of man.

At the Second Coming, man will be truly man, and men and women will experience a wholly other set of possibilities for the living of Life Eternal. Let them pray with the writer of Revelations: 'Amen. Even so; come, Lord Jesus!'

The Holy Mysteries

The Eucharistic worship of the Church is an activity in which both the Church on earth and the Church in heaven are engaged. They meet at the altar which is the heart of the total Church. The Holy Mysteries require an earthly celebrant but Christ himself presides as priest and victim. The Holy Mysteries are timeless and the Eucharist is a manifestation of the timeless in time.

The Church on earth is, as it were, the hands and feet of the Church in heaven upon which falls the greater burden of intercession and the exercise of the Divine Compassion. The unity between the Church on earth and the Church in heaven is absolute. The divisions of the earthly Church weaken and vitiate its witness among men for they are based, for the most part, on merely worldly criteria and are maintained by pride and vested interest. They are altogether transcended by that prior unity which cannot be broken between heaven and earth in Christ.

About the altar of God both heaven and earth meet. This is the point from which all commerce between them flows. It is the gate of heaven through which passes a two-way traffic, the purpose of which is finally to unite heaven and earth.

Man has no images available to his mortal mind with

47

which to articulate the realities of which he is partaker. Everything must therefore seem partial to him, and nothing complete. The waking consciousness lacks whole dimensions, therefore there must seem, at times, a measure of unreality in something which he cannot comprehend in terms of everyday life. He must walk by faith and not by sight, but sight will be given to him; even in this life he may have glimpses which will maintain and sustain him in his pilgrimage. And he may come to an awareness in part of the Communion of Saints and the fellowship of the Mind of Christ as he grows in participation.

The end product of that process which, in terms of human history, began with the Incarnation and will end with the Second Coming, is in fact a new and glorious beginning. As the process is timeless but impinging upon time it may be understood as drawing time into timelessness and redeeming the present moment into Eternity. It is impossible to pin down these realities in terms of merely intellectual categories, and intellectualism will have the greatest difficulties with them.

Eternity is a word which many men and women find awesome and even frightening. It has an abyss-like quality and it suggests earthly time extended to the power infinity. This is not a helpful image. Timelessness is perhaps a better word. Life is beginningless and endless; it simply *is* because God *is*. The dimensions which are unimaginable now will be commonplace and obvious in their simplicity then. The infinite richness and variety of creation is beyond all possibility of comprehension. It will be enough to wonder, to enjoy and to adore. These reactions are already appropriate to men and women on earth. How much more will they be appropriate in heaven!

The Christ will come in power and great glory. These are the keynotes of the Second Coming. Power is the power of total, self-sacrificial love triumphant. Great Glory is the revelation of the Divine Joy in all things.

Mortal men and women must learn to live and continually

abide with their minds in their hearts. They must know themselves to be sinners and without any merits other than the infinite merit bestowed upon them by God who made them, redeemed them and who calls them into the fullness of heaven for the love of them.

Mortal men and women must learn to see God in each other and to know themselves and each other to be in God. The context of their being is an Eternal Love Affair known to Christians as the Everblessed Trinity. They must know themselves to be each of an infinite worth in the love of God and persons of the one being, man. What men or women experience, be it good or ill, blessed or cursed, mystical or workaday, is the experience of man as a whole. The condition of the Whole is shared by each one, and in their midst, whose totality transcends both heaven and earth, in the Incarnate Lord. Of His Godhead all mankind are, in potential, partakers by adoption. Of the manhood of every man and woman he is partaker through the Blessed Virgin Mary, Mother of God.

Jesus came to begin the process of the union of God and man which his own Incarnation brought into being. He founded no new religion, for his coming signified the end of all religion. There is no temple in the heavenly Jerusalem. The Church is a people spread throughout heaven and earth. She is *Alter Christus* in her every member and partakes of the Mind of Christ, however partially in this life and however sinful and fallible she may be on earth. Her task is to herald the Second Coming. Her Eucharistic worship invokes the Saving Mysteries of her faith, and in her whole being she is a living prayer: 'Amen. Even so; come, Lord Jesus!'

PART TWO

Man, the Creator

Man is created in the image and likeness of God. The mind of man is creative and he was created in order to be a co-creator with the Creator of all. Creativity is the essential characteristic of all God's creatures, for even the most primitive are involved in creative activity according to their order. This is observable in terms of life upon earth. It is also the case on every other plane of being or mode of existence in the totality of a creation which is infinite and infinitely expanding.

In the creation myths of Holy Scripture, Adam partakes in the creating of the lower orders of being. In the myth, God brings every creature he makes to Adam who bestows upon it its name. The idea of the 'name' is profound. The name is the summing-up of the very being of the creature that is named. In the myth, that work of finishing off and completing the creating activity of God is left to man. Man is thus a co-creator with the God who created him.

Man is also God's steward, or manager. The earth is in the charge of man. Man must give account of his stewardship. Man is of the earth, earthy; a part of earthly creation and is the 'mind' and reflective consciousness of the earth. Man is thus a priest and stands at the point at which the earth and the Wholly Other meet, for there is that about man which is itself 'other'. In his priesthood he is isolated in part both from the earth which bore him and the heaven to which he aspires. He is the gateway between the two worlds and exists not for himself but for all other creatures, and for God.

This, expressed in the scriptural mythology, is what Man is, and what man is for; steward, manager, priest and co-creator with the Creator of all.

A man or a woman must create or die. Creativity is of the essence of human life and that is why those who neglect or suppress the talents that are given to them come under such fierce condemnation in the Gospel. Men and women are to foster and encourage each other's talents, not in a spirit of ego-centred competition, but out of a loving regard for the true *becoming* of the other person.

Creation, invention, adaptation and improvement are a sacred duty in all men and women, according to each one's ability, gifts and circumstances. Such are the vicissitudes of earthly life that it is rarely possible to pursue more than a fraction of a man's possible interests or to develop more than a fraction of his creative potential. But so long as the attempt is made, the responsibility recognized, nothing is lost for life is eternal. The man or woman who is too idle or indolent to attempt to create or to exercise the gifts given has abdicated life itself and will slowly die from within.

The imagination of every man and woman must be stimulated from earliest childhood. It is from within that all human creativity proceeds and a dulled or under-stimulated imagination will produce little to enrich either its own life or the lives of others. These things are vital. They are of the essence of the stewardship of man, his responsibility to manage the earth, and to be its priest to the Most High God.

That state of affairs which theology calls Original Sin means that Man has a defective will and a compromised integrity. His creative genius will therefore be put to ignoble and evil ends. This is the consequence of the fall from grace. But the responsibility to create remains. He may misuse his creative gifts just as he misuses the earth itself. He may create in part towards his own destruction, but create he must or he will die.

The creativity of the individual enriches the creative potential of all men. Creative potential is a perpetually

54

expanding attribute of mankind. The thirst for knowledge and understanding of the earth and of that part of the universe observable from earth and in earthly terms, is a fundamental attribute of the steward, the manager, the priest. Man's responsibilities are ever-expanding as he pushes the frontiers of his understanding further and further. This, in itself, is a faithful exercise and thoroughly consistent with the God-given vocation of mankind on earth.

Man's compromised integrity leads him deeper into difficulties with every advance he makes. The profounder his knowledge and capability become, the more potentially disastrous is his misuse of his faculties. But there is no escape from this dilemma. Man must go on if he is not to die from within. He runs an ever-greater risk of destroying himself by his own misdirected inventive genius.

There is no escape from this dilemma on a merely earthly level, but man's life is lived in an infinitely wider context and the problems of earthly life are, for any man or woman, of short duration. Mankind is essentially the same on earth or in heaven. Creativity does not cease with earthly life; very far from it! Those who have been faithful with the talents given to them will known an infinitude of creative and fulfilling potential. Those who have died within through idleness and indolence will know the error of their ways. Man is God's steward, manager, priest, on all planes or dimensions of being. The possibilities are endless, the responsibilities infinite, and the fulfilment and the Joy are altogether beyond all possibility of earthly comprehension.

Investigation, invention and creation are the hallmarks of human life. They manifest in earliest childhood and they are to be fostered and encouraged while life on earth lasts. To neglect them is to be unfaithful to life itself. Even the morbid products of misdirected invention are valuable, for nothing that Man makes is evil of itself. Only the perverted will of man is evil and every activity of mankind is capable of a blessed or a cursed application.

Man's awareness of his fallen state frightens him as he approaches the apparent mechanics of life itself. Men and women are aware of the awesome capacity for perversion and mischief of which they are capable, and are fearful of unleashing monsters upon themselves which they will be unable to control. There is no escape from this dilemma. To cease moving forward in investigation, invention and creativity is to abdicate humanity, even though the movement forward seems to lead inexorably to the abyss.

It is good to re-establish proven values that have become neglected. It is good to return to simplicity. It is good to become as little dependent upon possessions and gadgets as possible. But it is impossible either to stop the clock or make it go backwards. An invention cannot be un-invented. What Man has made he must live with; and he must by all and every means seek to turn it to good account and the glory of God.

Mankind's earthly life, therefore, is a pattern of growing and ever-deepening dilemmas. Man leaves a trail of wreckage behind him wherever he goes which the earth slowly transforms into a part of its landscape. Man's inventions become a part of the landscape; they are born, they live out their cycle and they die. The inner impulse, the creative inspiration passes into the everyday life of man as a whole and nothing is lost. The dilemma remains, gathering weight with every generation that passes.

The inventive curiosity of man drives him to investigate his own being in so far as he is able to do so. This investigation is pursued at many different levels. The human body, as a mechanism, is profoundly examined and there is a vast and growing corpus of knowledge and understanding about it. Certain of the workings of the human mind are similarly understood, but as it is a case of the human mind examining itself, the bounds of possibility and objectivity are more restricted.

The inner nature of man and what might be regarded as

his inner context are similarly under urgent investigation, under such headings as esotericism, magic, psychotherapy and mysticism. There is a built-in investigative drive which compels men and women to investigate, innovate and create. It is central to their very humanity and it matters little at what level or to what degree of sophistication it operates; the very operation of it is bound up with human life itself.

But man is a creature of compromised integrity. The temptation is ever-present to misuse, to manipulate, to embezzle, to pervert. And so all man's investigations into his own being are fraught with hazard, some of them of nightmare proportions. But there is no calling a halt to the process. Man creates or he dies. He must go on even though he runs the risk of self-destruction. The dilemma cannot be avoided; it is ever-present.

Law seeks to bring order into chaos by regulating what may be done and how far it may go. Law seeks to protect man from himself, to constrain and compel men and women to respect their neighbours. Law is always a failure for it is the attempt of the corrupt to regulate corruption and is thus ever-vulnerable to being corrupted. This is the human condition. Fortunately, earthly life is but a part of Life as a whole!

Man's dilemma is beyond resolution. He must investigate, innovate and create or die. His integrity is compromised and therefore his creativity is inexorably perverted to his threatened ruin. Untold millions of men and women have died because of man's perverted genius. Untold millions have lived and been restored to health by the same. The balance sheet is beyond human calculation and God alone is the auditor.

The Word became Flesh and dwelt among us. Man's perverted genius has ascended, with his humanity, to heaven and sits at the right hand of the Father. The context of human life and creativity is infinitely wider than mortal man can comprehend, and earthly life is neither the beginning nor the end.

Mankind must therefore stumble on, faced with a mounting dilemma with every new initiative, discovery or invention. The only way to escape the apparent abyss is to drive on through it in faith, for Christ has won the victory and, come what may, 'All shall be well, and all manner of thing shall be well'.

The Mind of Christ, into which mortal man is called, perfects and informs a man's or woman's creative gifts and drives. To begin to exercise this stewardship from within the Mind of Christ is to begin to reach beyond the ever-pressing dilemma. But in terms of earthly life it can never be the complete solution for mortal man can only partially partake of that Mind. His entire earthly pilgrimage is, at best, a slow growth by grace towards and into it, with many lapses and much error.

Mankind is a sinner by definition. Who need be surprised therefore that his stewardship is compromised, his creative genius perverted and his best endeavours tending always to his destruction? This is what sin is all about. It is from its ultimate consequences that he is saved.

The creativity of man extends beyond the bounds of this mortal life. It were not enough for life on earth alone to be the total context of a creature called by God to stewardship of such a high order. In Christ, that stewardship is extended, in potential, to the totality of creation.

An awareness of the wider context puts man's stewardship on earth into perspective. In his earthly context, man makes his mistakes and lives with them. The process of learning, for individual men and women, is of great length and of considerable trauma. It would be unrealistic to suppose that the span of one lifetime on earth would be sufficient, but it is unprofitable for mortal man to speculate beyond his own mortality.

The dignity of man is beyond his imagination. A sinner by definition, without any worth of his own, he is redeemed and called to an inconceivable glory. The Christ wills, as St Paul reminds us, 'to be the eldest among a large family of brethren'. To this dignity it is impossible to aspire. It is given freely; it cannot be sought. The potential for investigation, invention and creation is infinite. The faithful man or woman who has 'won the victory', as the author of Revelations puts it, has an ever-unfolding potential of fulfilment to look forward to. Man is called to be god with God; not by his own merits which are none, but by the freely offered gift of grace. Mankind is to be deified, and the process began at the Incarnation when the Word became Flesh and dwelt among us.

Meantime, in his life on earth, man moves uncertainly forward, uncovering ever more awesome possibilities and the responsibilities that attend them, conscious of his compromised integrity and ever reminded of the abyss into which he may, at any moment, fall.

The Mind of Christ is the true mind of Man. Only from within that Mind is it possible for man to fulfil his stewardship, on earth or in any other context. Man is struggling with his fallen state throughout his earthly life. His task, for which he was created and called out of the dust of the earth, is to be its reflective mind and its articulating voice of praise and glory to its Creator. This is of the essence of stewardship. Man is God's manager, managing creation for the sake of both Creator and created in personal self-forgetfulness. This is also of the very essence of priesthood.

This is the vocation into which every man and woman is born. This is their meaning and the whole purpose of their being. A man must grow into an awareness of responsibility. In the last resort, sin is a failure to be responsible. Man is a sinner by definition, and this means that there is a built-in tendency towards irresponsibility and betrayal of trust in him. The story of the Garden of Eden illustrates this splendidly.

There is in every man and woman a built-in tendency to expect a high standard of responsibility in others, but to make excuses for self. To grow in Grace is to bear an ever-increasing burden, both of personal responsibility and also of the evaded responsibility of others. To begin to participate in the Mind of Christ is to bear an ever-increasing weight, and it is the weight of the Cross. For Christ was crucified for being truly responsible, and for being thereby intolerable to the irresponsible. The mythological Atlas, with the weight of the world on his shoulders, is a type, a foreshadowing, of Jesus Christ, and of any Christian in mortal life who by the Grace of God comes to any profundity of participation in the Mind of Christ. But this is the calling of Everyman. The bearing of the world is what man was created for. He is redeemed in Christ to bear not just the world, but the total Universe.

The inventive genius of man must be fostered from his earliest childhood. This is a necessary part of the fulfilment of the stewardship of every individual, but it has a cumulative effect upon succeeding generations at many levels. A man must be faithful in small things before he can be trusted with larger ones. Inventive enthusiasms, easily dismissed as 'leisure activities', are a vital part of the wholeness of any man or woman and are neglected at their peril.

The humanity of vast numbers of men and women is inhibited and restricted, partly by circumstances, mostly by inherited or imposed prejudices and social patterns. Faithful stewardship demands a largeness, a fullness, a completely human manhood or womanhood, and the pattern for this is the Incarnate Lord himself.

God the Holy Spirit, working from within the innermost depths of a man or woman, is the primary instigator of the investigative, inventive and creative genius in man. These activities are at once human and Divine. In so far as mortal man is a fallen creature with compromised integrity, much of his genius is perverted to ignoble and destructive ends. This is the work of his diminished humanity, but it is still more faithful to investigate, invent and create than to fail to be thus human through fear of the consequences of success. The built-in dilemma is the human condition which has to be accepted as the consequence of the Fall, and lived with. By the action of Divine Grace all is transmutable by Love into means of Grace and fulfilment, so long as man is penitent.

To live is to create. This is the pattern of the life of the Holy Trinity in so far as it may be understood by creatures. Creation is an overflowing of love. The creaturely creativity of Man proceeds from the same overflowing of love. To be, therefore, is to create and the perversions of man's creative gifts are a perversion of love. This again is what is meant by man's fall from grace.

When the Word became Flesh and dwelt among us, Perfect Love became Incarnate and the entire human race was changed thereby. The potential thus established has to be realised, not only in every individual human life, but in man as a whole. Men and women are persons of the one being, man. What they do and what they suffer is done and suffered by man. What Jesus Christ suffered was the self-hating, self-destroying suffering of man. There is nothing beyond the possibility of redemption and transformation.

The exercise of the creative gifts is faithful stewardship. It is not possible to un-invent inventions which threaten to destroy their inventor. It is not possible to shrink from further investigation and discovery. Laws and regulations are temporary expedients by which the more destructive effects of man's disordered integrity are, to a certain extent, contained. There is but one remedy, however. Men and women must seek the aid of Divine Grace and slowly begin to participate in the Mind of Christ. The deeper their participation the more closely their free wills will conform to the Will of God, and their minds display something of the character of the Mind of Christ. Only thus can a man's or a woman's stewardship of the earth be faithful. Only thus can they come to the fullness of the stewardship of the Universe. That stewardship is heaven indeed.

The Silence of Heaven

The silence of heaven is made up of an infinite variety of sounds. Every creature in heaven or on earth sings a song of love to its Creator. The sum of all the songs is Silence.

Silence is not, therefore, an absence of noise but the ultimate harmony of all sounds. Noise, on the other hand, is the sound made by creatures in torment and is therefore distressing and destructive both of silence and of the peace that must abide in the inner depths of creatures if they are to be healthy. Noise is the sound of disintegration and it disintegrates creatures. Silence is the harmony of total integration and it integrates creatures because it is itself a grace to them.

It is not, in the main, those creatures which man regards as sentient which sing the most faithfully. Inanimate creation (as man regards it) sings, and it is possible for men and women to become aware of it, if they can become sufficiently silent within. Those who live among mountains are most likely to hear the song of silence on earth.

All the sounds of nature are part of the song. A man or woman who lives among the sounds of nature is a privileged being. Those condemned to live in great cities are deprived of a means of grace in the natural order of things, and yet natural beauty and harmony can work miracles of transformation in the depths of the urban wilderness and touch the hearts of many who would otherwise be deprived of part of their very humanity.

Man is a part of nature and he too has a song to sing, but

62

he is called to a dignity which bestows upon him the creation of his own harmonies. The music of Man is part of his priesthood and is a largely unconscious distillate of the harmonies all about him, presented to God as the fruits of His own stewardship.

Silence is the sum total of sounds in perfect harmony. A traveller in the desert, because of the barrenness and simplicity of his outward circumstances, is able to hear the sounds all about him, especially at night. The stars are audible to the human ear if only the ear will listen. Silence, like peace, is a harmony. The disturbing sounds, the alien sounds, are those that are not part of the harmony.

Silence is therefore something that may be heard and entered into. It is not possible to isolate the sounds of silence because they are parts of a perfect whole. Silence is to be entered into, not dissected. And a man or woman who enters into silence is on the one hand opening up the self to a massive means of grace, and on the other hand entering into great turmoil, even torment, for the dischord within will grow and become deafening in such a context.

External silence and internal silence enable and complement each other in a man or woman. To live with the mind in the heart is to have achieved a measure of inner silence which transcends the clamour and dischords of earthly life. To enter into a time of freely-willed silence is to enable the mind to find the heart where, by the grace of God, it may come to abide.

Silence and compassion march hand in hand. To enter into a time of silence with others is to become vulnerable to them and to have petty irritations to the ego revealed on the one hand, and to discover a new compassion for one's associates on the other. All torments are within. Between persons, a hitherto unsuspected *rapport* and mutual compassion can appear. Conversation seldom penetrates to the heart like a shared silence. In silence it is possible to be fitfully aware of something of the song that other hearts are singing to God, and to discover a measure of harmony with the song, unheard, in one's own heart.

The song that creatures sing comes from their hearts. By 'their hearts' is meant the deepest and most fundamental level at which they exist. This is not knowable to any but God. All creatures, man included, exist at many different levels and on many different planes of being. These things are a mystery and speculation about them is seldom other than misleading.

The many persons of man are spread throughout heaven and earth, and it is not helpful to speculate about that either. It is enough to accept it in Faith as a consequence of the Word having become Flesh and dwelt among us. A man or a woman must each discover his or her own song. All are different, all are unique, and when discovered each becomes part of the total harmony.

To discover his own song, a man must empty himself. This is a work of grace. He must discover his own deepest and truest nature and accept it. It is seldom what he expects or what his social conditioning might lead him to chose. Having discovered, he must live what he has discovered or he betrays his deepest nature. Divine Grace is always sufficient if only a man or a woman will believe and lay hold on it. The living of what a man is does not necessarily involve massive readjustment, but for some it does. This can be traumatic and can alienate a man from family and friends in some circumstances. But the criteria involved are wholly other than the criteria of the world.

To every man and woman comes a moment of truth. To some it is a gradual arrival, an indication of a trend in their innermost affairs. To others it is dramatic and traumatic. In all cases the timing of the moment and its decisions is crucial and must be left in the hands of the Holy Spirit who will stir a man or a woman towards decision when God's time for them is ripe.

Silence is the perfect harmony of all things in heaven and earth. The difference between heaven and earth exists mainly in the disordered mind of man.

For any man or woman, heaven begins on earth. It is first and foremost a state of mind and of being. It cannot be simply identified with the Mind of Christ, nor can it be only described as a state of mind and of being; but these are helpful ideas if not pressed too far. Heaven is a state of affairs and harmony is a state of affairs. Silence is therefore a supreme characteristic of heaven, but if this statement is to be made it must be interpreted positively, not negatively. The silence of heaven is not the silence of the tomb but the stillness and the joy of the Resurrection.

The silence of heaven must penetrate to a man's heart. This is a work of Divine Grace and is impossible in what is conveniently described as the natural order. Divine Grace perfects and transfigures nature, and what is impossible for man, is possible for God. A man must *become* silence. The man who does become silence is a messenger of peace in his very being. However loud and disorderly his worldly context may be, he will be peace and ensue it. In such a one, heaven is manifested among men, though man himself may never be aware of it and will shrink from the possibility of it because he will know himself to be a sinner.

Earth is a part of heaven. The world is tragically other. Men who are of the world are without the possibility of silence and are far from heaven. Men and women must leave the world and become citizens of earth if they are to know the fulfilment of heaven. Heaven is very 'down to earth'. To enter heaven, men and women must have their feet firmly on the ground.

Silence belongs to the heart and anything that speaks of silence touches the heart. All communication at its deepest level takes place within the silence of which those communicating are participators through their own songs.

The silence of heaven is a living and creative dynamic. In silence all that exists came into being. Silence is the supreme characteristic of the Mind of God, in so far as creatures may appreciate the Mind that thinks them, and articulate their experience of its energies. All things came into being out of the silence; they were born in total harmony, each singing its own song from the moment of its conception.

65

But all things are eternal; creation is beginningless and it is endless. It is the song that the creature sings which brings the creature itself into being, for it is the song that is first sung in the silence, and the song manifests as a creature.

Thus it is that the Holy Angels, if asked, describe themselves as music. They know what they are and from whence they came. Men and women are never closer to their angel brethren than when making music and enabling creatures to sing their songs through them.

The earth sings through the men and women who are its priests. The folk music of the world is the articulated song of the earth itself mediated through men and women who are close to the earth, and love the earth as their brother, their mother and their friend. All this is part of the silence of heaven; transmuting the sorrow of the world into Joy.

The silence of heaven is dynamic. For a man or a woman to enter consciously into that silence is for them an experience of profound renewal and redirection. Silence begets silence and calls out of men and women their own inner silence.

God the Holy Spirit is, in his energies, the sum total of silence. He is the silence of heaven because He is the Life of all things. It is not possible to say more because the Mystery, although able to be known and partaken of, cannot be defined or in any way known about.

God the ever-blessed Trinity is encountered and known in his energies but is unknowable in his essence. Silence, and all that goes to make it up, is a profound creative energy of God and all that runs contrary to, or is disruptive of the silence is self-destructive and tending always to evil. Silence is therefore intolerable for many men and women, for they are so conditioned to the disharmonies of evil that they begin to disintegrate in silence.

Disintegration is, in many respects, a form of necessary

demolition which must often come before rebuilding or re-creation. In man as a whole, the silence of Holy Saturday following the Crucifixion, was a necessary preliminary to the Resurrection. All this was suffered by Jesus Christ for the totality of mankind. Silence is often terrifying for it seems to be an abyss; but the abyss must be faced and a leap of faith made. This is a constantly recurring challenge for anyone seeking to enter into the silence of heaven, and it manifests on many levels and in many different ways for as long as earthly life lasts. The abyss is only afterwards revealed as part of the silence itself.

Every creature sings its own song to God and every creature has its own built-in rhythms. Rhythm and harmony together constitute the Great Dance which is Creation in the Mind of God.

All creatures are dancers in the Great Dance. The sum of their songs is the harmony and the sum of their rhythms is the rhythm of the Dance. And both together constitute the silence of heaven.

Creation is dynamic, and rhythm rather than form dictates the way in which a creature expresses itself upon every plane of being. The folk-dances of men and women give conscious expression to that which is going on at every level and upon every plane of being. The dance is a liturgy for man, offering the Great Dance to its Creator and Sustainer.

The Word, who became Flesh and dwelt among us, is Lord of the Dance and sets to every creature in heaven and on earth, and all creatures dance with him.

The Great Dance is the supreme energy of the Ever-blessed Trinity in so far as man can comprehend it. The Great Dance is the dynamic of creation and goes on for ever and ever. It is beginningless and it is endless. It transcends both time and timelessness, and the whole of mankind in heaven and upon earth is caught up in it.

The whole of human life relates to the Dance for the Dance is Life itself. To sing and to dance are the supreme attributes of humanity. To create songs and to create dances are the works of gods, and man is made in the image and likeness of God, and is co-creator with the Creator and Sustainer of all.

The Eucharistic worship of the Church is the Great Dance made manifest on earth. Its celebration invokes a solemnity which naturally expresses itself in ritual, however restrained. Ritual is man's attempt to grasp the truth that the whole of life is a dance, and that those things that speak to him most urgently of life and reality demand a solemn and ritualistic celebration.

It is not, however, ecclesiastical solemnity and ritualistic embroidery that constitute the Dance. The Dance is danced whenever the faithful meet in obedience to invoke the Saving Mysteries at the altar. The Lord who presides at His Mysteries is the Lord of the Dance. The Saving Mysteries are what the Great Dance celebrates, and the earthly celebrant is but a suit of clothes and a pair of hands and feet for the Lord of the Dance himself. Nobody is more aware of that than the celebrant of the Eucharist.

The Dance about the bread and wine, the Body and the Blood of Christ, given by Him to His Church, is danced both on earth and in heaven. The Eucharist is timeless and every celebration is a manifestation in time and space, in the here and now, of an Eternal Reality. The Church on earth and the Church in heaven are at one whenever the Dance is danced about an earthly altar. The Dance about the bread and wine is an invocation of the Fulfilment, the Parousia, the Second Coming of Christ in Glory. This is the concern both of heaven and of earth.

There shall be a new heaven and a new earth. They are both in being but their fullness is yet to be made manifest. The Dance is the invocation of this Mystery and the prayer of the Church both on earth and in heaven is that its fullness and its glory and its joy may be revealed, and that the Lord of the Dance may hasten the time.

Men and women are partners in the Dance. The principle of polarity is of universal application, and a man and a woman together sing a song which has its own harmony, which blends into the total harmony and becomes part of the silence of heaven.

The dance of man and woman is of infinite expression and gives the profoundest expression that creatures can give to the relationship of the Lord of the Dance to the rest of creation in general, and to each creature in particular. In this, each is, as it were, an icon: the man being the icon of the Creator, the Lord of the Dance, and the woman the icon of creation, the earth, the earth-mother, the Mother of God.

These icons are in part sacramental, in part role play. Men and women are equal. In mortal life they are essential to each other, but in heaven they are fully human, each one, 'as the Angels'. Nothing in all creation more perfectly reflects the beauty of the Divine Compassion than the mutual love, at all levels, of man and woman. Love is expressed in sacrifice. Sacrifice is expressed in the Dance. Their every gesture is a courtly self-giving. Courtship and affectionate flirtations have their place in any encounter between any man and any woman. It is the expression of respect and awe that each must have for the other.

The awe with which men and women regard each other derives from the Mystery of which both are a part but of which neither is the whole part. Of all the relationships in creation, that between man and woman is the most profound, the most tender and the most truly sacramental. Fallen mankind is incapable of its conduct without the help of God's Grace. Nowhere in the whole of human affairs are the effects of the Fall felt more painfully, and nowhere is mankind more tragically disfigured than at the central and most holy point at which the two halves of man's being meet in order to be One.

The silence of heaven is the perfect harmony of all the songs sung by every creature in creation. Thus it is a positive and creative silence, the perfect ambience for communication between creatures at every level and on every plane of being. It is life itself, the harmony of all the songs and the begetter of all the singers.

The silence of heaven is also the Great Dance, the perfect harmony of all the rhythms of the Universe in all its infinite dimensions. It is the ambience for the conduct of every relationship in heaven and upon earth, and between heaven and earth. The Lord Himself is the Lord of the Dance and occupies the centre of his own mental stage, dancing with all his creatures, collectively and individually.

The Lord of the Dance is the subjective Self of the Creator, projected into the midst of his own mental stage. He is subjective to the Father and objective to man and to the Holy Angels. But all this is a Mystery which can only be glimpsed in its energies and never in its essence.

The silence of heaven abides in the depths of the heart of man, and the hearts of men and women would fain abide within the silence of heaven and will not rest until they do so now, and for ever, and unto the ages of ages.

Meditation and Contemplation

Prayer is defined as standing before God with the mind in the heart. The form of prayer which most clearly conforms to this definition is Contemplation.

Meditation and Contemplation are two terms that are frequently confused, therefore they are here defined as follows: Meditation is a discipline of mental or interior prayer which makes use of images and symbols. Contemplation is a discipline of mental or interior prayer which abandons all images and symbols. In prayer, the discipline of meditation leads always in the direction of contemplation. Meditation as such is not necessarily prayerful and its techniques may be employed with many different ends in view, not all of them admirable. Nevertheless we are here concerned with prayer, and meditation will be treated as a discipline of prayer.

Meditation and contemplation reflect the two ways by which man may approach God. The first is the way of affirmation, the *via positiva*, in which God is perceived in his works and energies, and the human mind has something to get hold of. The second is the profounder way of 'unknowing'. For all that can be imaged or grasped by the intellect is other than God, and therefore the *via negativa* is concerned with laying aside all that God is *not*, until the abyss of unknowing is entered and, the soul being emptied, it is able to be filled with that of which it is impossible to speak or to comprehend other than with the comprehension of Love.

reverse in the east

71

Meditation is the prayer of the *via positiva*. It leads into the deeper prayer of contemplation which follows the *via negativa* in which the mind learns the habit of abiding in the heart. Contemplation brings a man into the timeless centre of his own being whence come all his truest inspirations and intuitions. Men and women must practice contemplation in order that they *become* contemplation. Meditation is an important step along this road.

Prayer involves the total person, therefore posture is important in order that the body may also pray and thus enable the mind to pray with greater recollection. The posture is important only in so far as it is comfortable, regular, relaxed and thus able to be forgotten. It is good that the spine should be erect and the head up. To allow the head to drop is to risk contemplating the navel. The psychosomatic links and associations are not always obvious but should not be ignored.

The use of symbols and images, and techniques of visualisation, are of the essence of meditation and there are as many variants as there are persons of the being, man. All these, combined with good, relaxed bodily posture, combine to bring the total being into recollection and, as symbol is the currency of the subconscious mind, to minimise the distractions which arise therefrom.

All this, of itself, is at a purely natural level. Divine Grace need not be involved, for these techniques, common to many cultures, are means of bringing the natural person under inner discipline. The inner world which meditation encounters is met with at a psychic level and it is important to understand this. There is nothing in the remotest degree truly *spiritual* in meditational technique, or in a great many of the uses to which it can be put. The silence that is induced is a psychic silence with certain of the properties of a vacuum. It is therefore necessary that the intention to pray to God be quite clear, and that meditation be entered into prayerfully with the desire to pass beyond it into the profounder state

72

of contemplation in which Divine Grace is fundamentally involved.

There are hazards attending the use of meditational techniques and they must be acknowledged, but they need not be feared if the firm intent is to pray to God and to rise beyond the level of the psyche until the mind, by Divine Grace, is fixed firmly in the heart.

Contemplation is an entering into silence. For mortal man it is hard work and requires total dedication and effort. Even with total dedication and effort, contemplation is at best patchy and partial without the aid of Divine Grace.

Unaided contemplation is brief and exhausting and cannot penetrate far into the heart. But the Divine Grace is ever available to those who are called to this way of prayer, and matches the total effort of a man with the grace of perseverence. By grace, a man can remain in silence, emptying his mind of all symbols and images until he discovers himself upheld, and sometimes transported, with all striving and effort suspended.

The transition from meditation to contemplation is made easier by the use of a mantram of which the most venerable is the *Jesus Prayer*:

'Lord Jesus Christ, Son of God, have mercy upon me, a sinner'.

This, repeated interiorly, is both a creed and an invocation. Its repetition will depend upon the individual, as will the exact manner of its use. But it must eventually sink into the heart in silence, carrying the mind with it until all is silence.

It is only by emptying out all that is not God from the heart and mind that the man or woman praying is able to be filled with *what God is*. Of this, nothing can be said. Only poetry can attempt an expression of this kind of Inexpressible, and only those who have some intuitive grasp of the Reality, or experience of a like kind, can really understand the poetry.

73

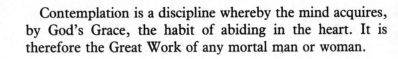

Contemplation is a discipline whereby the mind acquires, by God's Grace, the habit of abiding in the heart. It is therefore the Great Work of any mortal man or woman.

Practice

The practice of contemplative prayer has an immediate end in view and also a cumulative effect. The immediate end in view is to come into the Presence of God. A man is always in the Presence of God, so what is meant by this in the context of contemplative prayer is a fixing of the mind in the heart and the bringing of time into the timelessness of the centre of a man's being where God the Holy Spirit dwells.

All prayer, however articulated, is to the One, the Ever-blessed Trinity. Father, Son and Holy Spirit cannot be separated. God is God, and therefore nothing but confusion attends attempts to make God intellectually 'tidy'. The encounter with God is through – that is to say by virtue of – the humanity of Christ. Man encounters God in man-relatable terms. Thus the eternal Son of God is the Lover of all men and women. God the ever-blessed Trinity loves mankind through the humanity of Christ. The humanity of Christ is the point of *human* contact between man and the Wholly Other.

To abide with the mind in the heart, to lose time in the timelessness at the heart of man by the Grace of God, is to come into an awareness of God the Holy Spirit in the very depths, or equally accurately, the very heights of a man's being. This awareness is made possible by and through the humanity of Christ. As God is one and indivisible, the encounter is with the Risen, Ascended and Glorified Christ.

Contemplation is a way. Sometimes, according to a man's or a woman's vocation and needs, the Divine Grace transcends the slow process of maturity and brings the human soul into an awareness of, and a knowledge of, the Divine Presence. This can be an experience of the greatest trauma mixed with the greatest blessing. The profounder the experience, the longer the soul will take to come to terms with it in real depth. Ten years, twenty years and more, may be needed to progress from an immediate knowledge to mature, but yet partial, understanding. A lifetime is needed for the progression from understanding to wisdom.

Meditation is essentially a matter of techniques which are employed for a purpose. In prayer, the normal end in view is the attainment of contemplation. There are other prayerful uses of meditational techniques, however, which can be great means of Grace under certain circumstances and at the right time.

Meditation with the use of symbols, including the prayer use of the imaginary inner journey, can aid a man or woman to discover concealed truths concerning the self. This is not an undertaking that should be entered upon lightly as it can be frightening and profoundly disturbing. The technique of invoking symbols and undertaking imaginary inner journeys is essentially magical and must be recognized as such. Magic has been defined as the art of making changes in consciousness in accordance with the will. To employ symbols in meditation and to undertake imaginary inner journeys is to cause changes in consciousness to be made, but at a natural rather than at a spiritual level. However, the Divine Grace can enable this when the time is right and circumstances appropriate, and from the depths of what is conveniently described as the Unconscious, buried and long-forgotten truths about the self can emerge into the light of reason.

This, when appropriately entered into, can be a profound exercise in self-awareness, understanding, acceptance of self and compassion. As such, its fruits can be wholly good. There will come an instinctive awareness concerning the time to abstain from this kind of meditation, and employment of these techniques for reasons of self-indulgence or with the desire to manipulate is a practice fraught with all manner of hazard.

Men and women must learn to trust God. God the Holy Spirit, who dwells at the heart of man, is the profoundest psychoanalyst of them all. Everything that causes men and women to become self-understanding and self-accepting is of Grace, as their self-forgetting in contemplation will be profoundly assisted thereby.

Meditational techniques of various kinds can bring a man into silence; but mere technique, the training of the autonomic nervous system by *mantram* or *bija*, can of itself induce no more than a psychic silence. It is of the utmost importance to recognize this.

Psychic silence is, in many ways, a vacuum. It invites phenomena to fill it, and man, in the purely natural order, is limited in his capacity to discern. The psychically sensitive may be confident about the matter of discernment, but at the natural, psychic level the human mind cannot discern, among other things, objective evil. The possibilities of deception by wrongly discerned or completely undiscerned phenomena are very real among those who rely upon technique to bring them into psychic silence, and do not aspire to pray to God in contemplation.

It is of the utmost importance to distinguish between contemplation, which partakes of the silence of heaven, and psychic silence which is purely of the natural order. Among those who are naturally psychically sensitive, a naive identification of the psychic with the spiritual is widespread, and pride makes many reluctant to admit of the possibility of error.

Divine Grace does not operate in a vacuum, however, and Grace perfects and transfigures that which is of the natural order. It is a sad mistake, therefore, to eschew or to turn in fear from the psychic, which is a most important part of any man or woman. It must be accepted and affirmed, not rejected or denied. Truth and wholeness require the total person to be perfected by Grace. Meditational technique has a useful, and for many an important, part to play in their prayer. But the distinction between meditation and contemplation must be understood, the Grace of discernment prayed for, and the exercise of all these things done in the context of fervent prayer to God.

The silence of heaven, unlike psychic silence, is wholly positive with nothing about it of the vacuum. Contemplation is a self-emptying by grace in order that the whole being may be filled and may *become* that with which it is filled.

Contemplation is supremely the discipline of giving to God the undivided attention of the will. This requires total concentration and maximum effort, but its success depends upon Divine Grace. The human effort, made by the will, is matched by that which enables it to persevere and to attain its end.

There are times of great trial and darkness during which the soul is purified and the will exercised to its limits. There is no desolation like the desolation of contemplation when contemplation appears to be altogether impossible. The prayer is conducted, however, not just at the level of conscious awareness but at a deeper level altogether, and the praying soul must persevere, come what may. Many great saints have lived for years at a time in this kind of darkness, so the suffering soul may rejoice in its good company!

Contemplation has nothing to do with phenomena as such, though to some people phenomena may manifest in their prayer. These are not important and this is a stage that will pass as all phenomena are transcended.

An intense awareness of the Divine Presence is sometimes experienced, and sometimes the person in contemplation is caught up in a manner described by St Paul, concerning which nothing more can be said. Occasionally the praying soul may be transfigured in the Holy Spirit, far in advance of any permanent state of grace. These are graces bestowed, and vocations and responsibilities attend them. But the basic nature of contemplation remains; the giving of the undivided attention of the will to Almighty God.

The mystical degrees of contemplation are graces that are given and cannot be aspired to. However, the object of Contemplation goes beyond mystical states of prayer and seems to come, full-circle, back to a child-like simplicity. The man or woman praying enters into an easy friendship with the Lord which seldom demands the great efforts of meditation and contemplative prayer. These are entered into when they seem to be appropriate. At all times the soul simply 'abides'.

The inner stillness, the silence of heaven, becomes a feature of life and never abandons the heart. The heart and the mind are at one, and an easy commerce takes place between heaven and earth. Prayer is simplicity itself, for the soul has come some way towards *becoming* prayer rather than doing it.

Contemplation is therefore unglamorous. Excitements belong to earlier stages in the life of prayer and the sooner they are transcended the better. The contemplative life may be lived in the cloister or in the world. Sometimes it demands something of each. All true and worthwhile activity stems from contemplation, for to live the contemplative life is to live with the mind in the heart, and it is from these heights, or depths, that the truest intuitions and inspirations come.

There is a penalty attached to the contemplative life. The soul who embarks upon this way will sooner or later encounter the realities of spiritual warfare and will come under unrelenting assault from an inner darkness which is other than the self. No more need be said on this subject, but the sufferings involved can be severe, even terrible. Love, however, expresses itself in suffering and nothing is beyond transmutation in love. Contemplation is the easy and ever-deepening relationship between lovers. It is an entry into, and an abiding within the Mind of Christ and is the work of Divine Grace upon the soul.

The Rosary

A meditational technique of proven worth, which bridges the gulf between meditation and contemplation, is the Rosary.

The traditional Rosary, with its five sections each of ten beads, with beads between the sections, is used as an aid to meditation upon three sets of five mysteries. These are the Joyful Mysteries, concerning the Incarnation; the Sorrowful Mysteries, concerning the Passion; and the Glorious Mysteries, concerning the Resurrection, Ascension and their implications. The fingering of the beads and the recitation of the *Ave Maria* as a mantram, involves both the body in prayer and also the superficial levels of the mind. This releases the deeper levels, either to meditate on the Mysteries, or to penetrate deeper into an inner silence that the telling of beads and recitation of the mantram facilitates.

The Rosary provides a screen of quiet activity which shields against the ever-present hazard of distraction. The telling of beads becomes almost an unconscious act and the *Ave* sinks into its own inner silence and the man or woman praying is enabled to go further and deeper in consequence.

The Mysteries themselves proclaim the Christian Faith, and a more superficial use of the Rosary will very usefully assist meditation upon them. But this simple technique of bead-telling in time with a mantram is of the greatest help in leading souls from vocal prayer, through meditation, into contemplation, and should not be despised by anyone.

The traditional mantram in Western Christendom is the *Ave Maria*. In the East it is the *Jesus Prayer*. It matters little which of the two is used. The Christian East has its own Rosary which is simpler. The important point is that this is a technique in prayer which helps to bridge the great gap between meditation and contemplation and is thus a powerful means of Grace.

Meditation is the prayer of the *via positiva*. Contemplation is the prayer of the *via negativa*. The first leads into the second; the first is an exercise of the rationality and the second an exercise of the intuition, leading to the whole person being in equilibrium, with the mind in the heart.

Prayer in any of its forms is a conscious living of a personal relationship with the Creator. It is a freely-willed giving to God of the undivided attention of the will in order that God the Holy Spirit may be set free to work within the total being. All prayer is enabled by the Divine Grace, for although men and women think themselves to be in search of God, in reality it is God who is in search of them. In order to be found, they must lose themselves.

The distinction between the psychic and the spiritual is crucial if a man is not to be lead astray after counterfeits which, though sometimes good in themselves, are not what he imagines them to be. The grace of discernment of spirits must be asked for, for not every spirit is of God and the discernment which is of the purely natural order is not adequate, however confident a man may imagine himself to be.

All who seek to pray earnestly and in depth come under the assault of powers of evil outside of themselves. These hazards must be accepted with confidence for Christ has won the Victory.

Life and the Living of it

The earth is the Lord's and the fullness thereof. Man, Scripture tells us, is made in the image and likeness of God. The same is true of every other creature according to its order.

Man's own creations reflect his personality, his character, the distinctive cast of the individual mind that brought them forth. The same is true of the Eternal Mind in which all things, at the deepest level of their being, are thoughts.

Man takes materials which are to hand and fashions his artefacts from them, imposing new patterns and an altered character upon the raw material and bringing it into a new category of being. Man realises the potential of much of creation, this is his vocation and responsibility. The creativity of God is Wholly Other in that there are no raw materials and all is created *ex nihilo*. But a little of this Mystery is revealed by man's discovery that there appears to be *no ultimate matter*. The deeper man goes in his investigations into matter, the more intangible it becomes until energy rather than matter appears to present itself and, in a famous phrase, the atom appears to be 'the structure of a set of operations'.

God is known, not in His essence, which is unknowable, but in His energies, and energy appears to present itself as the primary raw material of creation. The idea of creatures being, in some sense, thoughts in the Mind of God takes on a new meaning, for energy appears to organise itself and

81

manifest as matter. The idea of an underlying purpose behind these 'sets of operations', while still a matter of faith for any man or woman, begins to be credible in a new way. The implications for man are considerable, for he too is but the structure of a set of exceedingly complex operations and is himself but energy organised for a purpose.

Every creature in the whole of creation reflects, in some way, the character of its Creator, and physical creation (for want of a better description) is the manifestation of the essential *idea* as it is, and as it develops, in the Mind of God.

Man on earth is bound to deal with matter as if it is, in some sense, absolute. This is the only way by which he can relate to it, or indeed to himself, even though he knows in his heart that there is more, both to himself and to everything else, than outward appearances and everyday experience suggests. However, men and women are themselves manifestations of an archetypal *idea*. Remove that *idea* from this mortal life by death, and the disintegration and decomposition of the body begins immediately.

A man or a woman is not, therefore, a body possessed of a faculty or attribute called 'life'. A man or a woman is the *idea* of themselves at a level which is wholly other than any which they can imagine. It is the *idea* which manifests in this life through the processes of birth and growth to maturity. The *idea*, like all ideas, develops and changes; but being an idea in the consistent Mind of God it changes in a manner consistent with, and in character with, its origins. A human being, a person of the Being, man, is therefore recognizable and identifiable on any and every possible plane of being, for the person will manifest in complete consistency according to the circumstances of that plane of being.

This casts some light on the Resurrection. The total person IS, and shall forever remain. Nothing is lost and all is gained. The *idea* is eternal and eternally developing, and so the potential of the person is forever extended and extending. But the person is the same person, containing within its being both the masculine and the feminine, and in heaven neither marrying nor being given in marriage, but as the angels.

It is not possible for a mortal man to understand himself in very much greater depth than his normal conscious mind and rationality will allow. Therefore it is difficult, indeed well nigh impossible to behave in a manner consistent with the glimpses of heights or depths that are sometimes bestowed. A mortal man must use poetic images and models of all kinds to aid his comprehension. A working hypothesis must be arrived at and maintained for as long as it works. But images, models and hypotheses must not be allowed to harden until they become idols, for an idol is a model of God which reflects fallen man's values and is entirely man-made. Whatever truth it might have pointed to is now obscured by the specious divinity bestowed upon it.

All that has been said so far is, of necessity, poetic imagery or human model-making. The truths that these things point to are infinitely greater, the Love is more loving, the joy more joyful.

Nevertheless, the earth is the Lord's and the fullness thereof, and all creatures reflect the Creator and all are brethren. Man is brother to the rest of creation. As steward and manager of God's earth he is brother to the earth itself at all its levels, for all its levels are present in himself though most of them are beyond his conscious awareness in this life.

The risen and ascended Christ, Paul reminds us, desires to be the eldest of a large family of brethren. This is the pattern for man's own relationship with the creatures among whom he dwells and for whom he is responsible to God as steward and priest. This *idea* is made manifest in the Incarnation. This is the *idea* which was made manifest by the Word becoming Flesh and dwelling among us. By Divine Grace, men and women are slowly made able to live and behave as

83

brothers and sisters to each other, and to the rest of creation. The true relationship can only be realised by the Grace of God, but in this realisation, men and women become truly human.

The earth is the Lord's and the fullness thereof. Every creature in all creation is equal in the Love of God for love alone brought it into being. Love causes ideas to manifest. Love imparts structure and love directs operations. There is no other motivation in the Mind of God.

Love is wholly without sentimentality. It is objective and detached. Ideas are caused to manifest and allowed to get on with their business of being and becoming. The catastrophies change them and they develop from beginninglessness to endlessness. Nothing is static; all is dynamic.

On earth, man is both subject to catastrophe and also an author of it, both for himself and for his brethren. His brethren include the rest of sentient life; plants, the very earth he walks on and the very air he breathes. For all these he is responsible. They modify him and he modifies them. His every action has its own built-in consequences at many levels. He must live with the consequences of his actions. At the deepest level as far as mortal life is concerned he has to live with the moral consequences of his actions, and he is by definition a sinner.

Man's sinfulness is a consequence of the free-will given to him and his misuse of it. Man misuses everything that he is given. Everything is dedicated to a lesser good and he misses every opportunity that he is given. Man lives in the context of the lesser good; that is the consequence of his sinfulness. But the Word became Flesh, and so the lesser good which man created for himself is become a 'School for the Service of the Lord'.

Thus the unsentimental, objective and detached love which called man into being deals with the muddle he has made, and by the action of Divine Grace, men and women grow into that Mind of Christ in which alone it is possible to be truly human.

Truthful Conduct

Morality derives from the interaction of persons. Morality is concerned with the truthful conduct of persons towards each other. Men and women are in a personal relationship with each other, with all other men and women, and with God. It is the interplay of all these personal relationships that morality is concerned with.

Truthful conduct is self-forgetting; it is concerned with the wellbeing of the other, and of all others. It is concerned with giving others their due rather than receiving its own. In a society in which all persons conduct themselves truthfully there is perfect harmony, for all share a common mind of self-forgetting mutual compassion and understanding. But such a society does not exist among men and women on earth. It is breakdown which causes such a concept as morality to have any meaning. It is a failure of love which gives rise to law. Law and morality seek to bring order into a chaotic situation. They provide constraints and criteria but neither are effective at any depth.

It is man's sinfulness which causes men and women to sin. The lesser good is lesser because its criteria are ego-centred. All other persons, all other creatures, are reduced to the level of 'things', and the ego reigns as its own criterion and its own god. The consequences of this are baleful in the extreme, but to the rest of creation they are also baleful, for man is a spoiled priest, and one who has lost sight of the obvious truth that God is incapable by his very nature of creating anything in other than personal terms. He relates only in personal terms. Everything that exists, therefore, is to be known and understood, at some level, in personal terms. There is therefore a moral consequence in everything that a man or woman does, for everything in the whole of creation is a person, and there is no truthful relationship with anything other than the personal.

All things belong to God. All things abide in God. All things are full of God. A man may see his Creator anywhere in creation. All things are holy, but their holiness is the holiness of the God who made them. Creatures are by no means to be identified with, or confused with, their Creator.

A man's approach to his fellow men and women must be with awe and respect, for God is in them and visible through them, however misguided, wicked or depraved. A man may be given over to evil and live by his basest instincts and most primitive appetites, but he is still a man, made in the image of God, in whose inmost depths God the Holy Spirit dwells. The sinfulness of a man does not hinder his abiding in God or God's abiding in him. Wilful sin and a dedication to the lesser good, if not to outright evil, stunts his growth, withers him at the roots and destroys the chance given to him to become what he is.

A man's approach to nature itself must be with the same awe and respect for God is everywhere to be found. All things abide in God and God in them, but by no means are creatures to be identified with their Creator and worshipped. A man must love his fellows and the rest of creation for two qualities: the first is that God is in them and they in God, the second is their own creaturely integrity and uniqueness.

Love is, among other things, a mixture of affection and respect. Without respect a man cannot relate in truth to any others at all or they to him. Without affection he has not emerged from his own ego and even begun to live in a human way.

Human life cannot be lived without mutual affection and mutual respect. It is the misery of the fallen human condition in earthly life that the attempt is made to live without either. This is, quite simply, hell on earth.

The earth is the Lord's, and so are the heavens. The *idea* which lies at the heart of any creature manifests itself in a manner appropriate to itself and to its context. Thus the Angels of God obey the same basic rules as do men and women, but according to a different order. The *idea* of them is manifest in a manner appropriate to their integrity and their context. It does not do, however, for men to speculate much further about them. It is sufficient to acknowledge them as brethren.

A man or a woman who arbitrarily denies the existence of any creature of a different order to man, or of any plane of being other than that of mortal life of earth as normally experienced, suffers an impoverishment of tragic dimensions. Some men and women are naturally more sensitive to, and aware of, realities other than those regarded as normal. Other men and women are less sensitive to them, but the matter of sensitivity itself is of small importance. Arbitrary denial of the possibility of other creatures' existence, apart from its astonishing arrogance, is an impoverishment of the vision of those perpetrating the denial. Life is so much bigger, and richer, and more joyful. Man has a multitude of brethren to whom he has a duty to show compassion and respect. A mind which slams the door on possibilities beyond its experience does so in fear, and it robs itself of far greater possibilities in consequence.

Fear is the greatest impoverishment of all. It is fear, as often as not, which perverts relationships between persons. It is fear which causes sinful man to hide from the God who seeks him. Fear makes a man cruel to his fellow men, and fear causes a man to seek to deprive other creatures of their being. Fear is a consequence of the fall from grace, but perfect love casts out fear and enables a man to open his eyes in ever-increasing astonishment at the richness of creation and the spreading multitude of those who have compassion for him.

All life belongs to God and derives from God. Consciousness is a property of life and, to some degree at least, all things are both living and conscious. From the point of view of mortal man, both life and consciousness must appear to be potential rather than fully realised.

Man's own life and consciousness are very far from being fully realised for they come from beginninglessness and they go to endlessness. Man's consciousness, unique as he understands it in the world in which he lives, is reflective. A man can reflect upon himself with a measure of objectivity. This is what makes him human. But the Mystery of Life and the Mystery of Consciousness derive from the Creator and belong to Him alone.

This truth was grasped and celebrated in a primitive form in the Old Testament when blood, mistakenly identified with life itself, was treated with such awe that in sacrifice it was poured on the altar. Sacrifice sought to give God what belongs to God, in other words life itself.

Man has the stewardship on earth of life. He is able to take life, both from other creatures and from his own kind. This is his must awesome responsibility and that which has built into it the profoundest consequences. A man is always dealing with his brethren. It is always his brother whose life is in his hands, regardless of the level of development of the creature. Man is a sinner by definition. He is as likely to do wrong as to do right. Man-made laws hedge him in on every side, for the benefit of all, but law is always a failure and perpetually liable to perversion and corruption. Only from within the Mind of Christ can a man or woman make decisions regarding the stewardship of life on earth with any hope of truthfulness. Only one who has lost his life can appreciate life. Divine Grace alone enables faithful stewardship. But life is eternal and is never lost however man may sin, or regardless of the catastrophies of nature.

The quality of a man's life is largely in his own hands, in spite of outward circumstances. Quality has to do with the state of a man's heart rather than the state of his surroundings or the quantity of his goods and chattels. Nevertheless a man has a duty to enhance the quality of the lives of others, and to do all in his power to improve the general lot of all.

This, however, is not a political matter so much as a spiritual one. Political solutions, like law, belong to the world and men and women who are in Christ are called to be citizens of earth and heaven, and not of the world which is passing away. There will always be a dilemma, and Christians will not necessarily agree with each other as to how to better the general lot and in particular the lot of the poor, the downtrodden and the unfortunate. It will be as mistaken and blameworthy to do nothing as to do something when the something, whatever it is, will certainly be at least partially mistaken.

Man has a stewardship for man. All men and women are persons of the one Being, and when they come into destructive and greedy competition with one another they manifest the effects of the Fall in the starkest manner. Life on earth is full of contradictions and dilemmas, few of which are capable of resolution and all of which have to be lived with and struggled against. This is the exercise of stewardship in a humanity which is flawed and deformed in will.

Man is one being. The persons of man extend through heaven and earth. The totality of mankind contains the struggling few on earth at any one time. Life on earth is turned, by virtue of the Incarnation, into a 'School for the Service of the Lord'.

The earth is the Lord's and all that is within it. The heavens are also the Lord's. Life and consciousness belong to the Lord. All things begin and exist at their deepest level as *ideas* which manifest on earth, in heaven, on every plane of being and in the context of every combination of dimensions that exist.

All things are persons, for God is Person and cannot relate to His creatures in any way other than with the love of person for person. All things are alive and conscious in some way unknowable by mortal man and all things are therefore his brethren.

Man's stewardship extends throughout the earth and is exercised over brethren. He has the power bestowed upon him to take life. This decision is an exercise of his stewardship for which he must render an account. No life is lost for all life is God's. Man disposes on one plane of being only.

Man is responsible for man. Men and women are responsible for each other and for the quality of life that outward circumstances make possible. But all these things are spiritual

matters, belonging to the heart. A man or woman must live mindful of all these things. Only Divine Grace makes this possible. Only a mind abiding in the heart and at one with the Mind of Christ can possibly exercise stewardship with a hope of faithfulness.

Reason and Intuition

Theology is, quite literally, 'God talk'. It is man's attempt to come to terms with his experience of the energies of God. Theology derives from mystical experience; mysticism and theology go hand in hand for the latter is the interpreter of the former. The two represent the human faculties of Intuition on the one hand and Reason on the other.

In a fully integrated human being the faculties of intuition and reason will be in complete balance and harmony. Each will inform the other and also interrogate the other. Alas! There are no fully integrated human beings. Christ alone is fully human. Growth into full participation in the Mind of Christ, growth in Grace, brings a man or a woman slowly into the Way of Integration, but in this mortal life the best is but partial.

Theology and mysticism must always keep in the fullest touch with each other, both in an individual and also in the Church as a whole. A loss of contact between them will immediately unbalance an individual. A mystic – still worse an aspiring mystic – who is careless of theology, which represents the collective interpretation of the Church as a whole, is likely to be led by an untaught intuition in all manner of false directions. A rationalist, dismissive of mysticism and contemptuous of mystics, will find himself living an arid, two-dimensional life and is in danger of wandering from the Faith in a fog of intellectualism.

91

Theology is renewed in Contemplation. Contemplation is directed and sustained by Theology. Intuition and reason are like a man's two ears, two eyes, two hands, two feet. Without both he is incomplete; with one exalted and the other maimed he is a cripple.

There are three ways by which a man may come to an understanding of the ways of God with man. The first is the direct *knowing* of love; the experiential knowledge of God in his energies in what is commonly called mystical experience. This is given rather than sought. It transcends intuition but it is by the intuition that it comes to a man.

The second way of knowing is that of intuitive awareness. This proceeds from the depths of a man and is an instinctive knowing. It is not irrational but it is non-rational. It requires interrogation by the reason and reconciliation with reason.

The third way of knowing is that of reason. This requires interrogation by the intuition, for what seems reasonable is not always right, and the intuition can act as a vital corrective. Humanity in balance enjoys reason and intuition in close accord, but humanity is seldom balanced.

Reason and intuition translate the experiential knowledge of God into human terms and what emerges is known as theology. Thus the Eastern Church reserves the description 'theologian' for a tiny handful of the Saints in its calendar who were great mystics and also powerfully reasoned thinkers. The implications of the experiential knowledge of God translated into human terms are then considered in relation to everyday human life and the result of this consideration is called morality.

This, therefore, is the progression from revelation, through theology to morality. It will be seen that there is a 'stepping down' as if through a transformer at each level. But the three must be consistent with each other. By virtue of the fact that man is a sinner, inconsistencies may expect to be found. Nevertheless there is no other possible course of revelatory action, nor is there any other possible course of human response to it, however flawed the latter may be.

Christian Doctrine

Theology is about God. It is the discipline of reconciling revelation with reason. In the process it is obliged to image God in man-made terms and to construct doctrines, all of which are suspect in so far as they are human. However, there is no alternative. God is always greater than the most faithful doctrinal definition. Man is obliged to stand by the very best that his reason can produce and the basic doctrines of the Church are the least inadequate statements in human terms of the Divine Revelation.

Reason, when used prayerfully, is aided by Divine Grace. Intuition informs and questions. Between the two faculties, dedicated to God in prayer and offered for enlightenment, the truths of the Divine Revelation are articulated faithfully. Over the first few centuries of the life of the Christian Church a framework of doctrine emerged which enshrines the faith of the Church as a whole.

Within this framework of doctrinal statement and definition, individual Christians live and grow. Their reason must struggle with the unknowable. The Mystery strains against the definitions that have emerged. Faith is sanctified by doubt, and doubt is faced and struggled with. The doctrinal framework of the faith of the Church provides an arena for many a contest, a safe refuge, a strong wall to bounce ideas off and a context for growth in grace.

Within the security of the faith of the Church, defined in obedience to the revelation given and sustained through the ages, men and women grow by Divine Grace into the Mind of Christ who is himself the Revelation, and as such greater and more glorious than any doctrine can hope to articulate, however faithful.

Christian doctrine has evolved in response to two quite separate stimuli. The first was the experience of Jesus in his earthly ministry and the continuing experience of Jesus in the life and liturgy of the Church. The implications of experience, of Divine Revelation in Jesus, had to be faced, struggled with by the collective reason of the Church, and articulated. The second stimulus was a succession of false definitions and premature doctrines which, if accepted, would have perverted and distorted God's Truth as it was revealed in Jesus. The great heresies had to be recognized as such and doctrinal definitions arrived at which safeguarded the Truth against them.

The great heresies all arose from human cleverness seeking to run ahead of itself. Intellectualism cannot grasp the wholeness of the faith for it lacks essential dimensions and is dismissive of the intuition. Orthodox Christian doctrine derives from a great labour of the collective reason of the Church, backed up by an equal labour of the intuition of the Church, both enabled by Divine Grace.

Mystery, however, is incapable of definition and so doctrinal definitions are themselves inadequate and must be recognized as such. The Truth is always greater, the Glory more glorious and the Joy more joyful.

Intellectualism repeats the same venerable heresies in every generation yet declines to admit the fact. It is always dismissive of intuition and always lacking in essential dimensions. It emasculates the Faith and radically inhibits its own practitioners from experiencing any of the realities of which it is dismissive. The loss belongs to the intellectualist alone, but an intellectual ambience of this sort can be temporarily harmful and inhibiting to other Christians because it is a denial of the wholeness, not only of the faith, but of humanity itself, and all in the name of human cleverness. It was to safeguard the faith and the faithful that Christian doctrine was eventually defined.

Mysticism

Intuition requires a rigorous interrogation by the reason if it is to be fully human in its operation. An intuitivism undisciplined by the reason is as mischievous as rationalism untempered by intuition. Intuitivisms tend to construct their own premises with scant regard for the intellect. The result of this is quite subhuman.

Mortal man is quick to exalt his perceptions, be they intuitive or rational, into 'isms'. It is not too much to say that warfare between these 'isms' has done more damage to men and women than any other agency in the last one thousand years. A man must sit lightly to the hypotheses he constructs. All his perceptions, at whatever level, are partial, fleeting, fragmentary and flawed. None more so than those of the intuition which is unbalanced and not subject to discipline by the reason.

Mysticism, without a sound basis in theology, can practically be relied upon to lead men and women astray, remove their feet from the ground and deteriorate into magic and psychism. The so-called esoteric realm is exalted to an 'ism' and invaluable insights and important truths are discredited through being spuriously 'deified'.

Theology, without a firm and continuing basis in mysticism, becomes an arid intellectualism which loses touch with God who is its purpose, and wanders in an intellectual jungle of the bright ideas of clever men until it has lost all touch with the faith which inspired it, or with the lives of men and women who pray to God.

Man is a sinner by definition. Both these mischievous possibilities are in every man and woman and manifest, to some degree, either in one way or in another.

Faith

Faith itself is a gift of God. The faith which is of nature, that is to say the faith of which a man is capable, is a feeble thing but its stirrings are supported by the Grace of God which raises faith to a new and transcendent level.

As St Paul reminds us, we walk by faith and not by sight. Men and women on earth are invited to live by trust in God and in the loving providence of God. The Christian revelation is accepted in faith and can only be entered into from faith. This is necessary for man who is a creature of free will and has the privilege of possible disbelief.

Doubt is often regarded as a sin. It is feared. To lose one's faith is a terrible thing, and it is certainly a tragic misfortune for it is akin to blindness. However, doubt is a necessary possibility. It is also a means of Grace if accepted and offered honestly. Men and women often grow in the faith through the ministry to them of doubt. Doubt must be faced positively and fearlessly. Doubt, in other words, must be suffered faithfully! It can then act as a purgative and cleanse the system of unimportant clutter, and enable questions that need to be transcended rather than answered to die away and a greater truth to emerge.

Faith must be reconciled with reason. Faith is not a product of reason but more nearly a product of the intuition. It must, sooner or later, be understood by the believer as reasonable and credible. An irrational and emotional approach to faith is unhealthy and insecure. It savours less of love than of sentimentality which is a morbid counterfeit of love.

Faith is a gift of God. So is the reason. The two must become one.

Morality

Morality derives from the attempts of the reason to come to terms with Divine Revelation. All relationships between Creator and creatures are personal. Man enters into a personal relationship with his Creator. Men and women relate to each other and to all other men and women in a person-to-person relationship. Man relates to the rest of creation in a person-to-person relationship, even if he is unaware of the fact; even if he denies it.

Morality has to do with person-to-person relationships. Were man not a sinner there would be no need for morality, for love would determine all things. But man is a sinner, and the conduct of his relationships is disordered. Morality is the vision, as seen through the eyes of a sinner, of how things should be.

Moral codes are the product of the reason. The reason has come to terms with an encounter with the Wholly Other. Theology is the articulated result of this coming to terms, and morality has derived from it as a natural and reasoned consequence.

This can be seen in the story of Moses receiving the tablets of the Torah. Divine Revelation in a mystical experience is symbolised by the story of the hand of God carving the Law on tablets of stone. But Israel could not receive this as the heart of Moses received it. They were sinners and engaged in unfaithfulness, so Moses threw down the tablets of stone engraved by the hand of God, and carved two more with his own hand. These are traditionally identified with the Ten Commandments, a rule-book of 'do's and don'ts'.

Moses was therefore a 'transformer', stepping down the Divine voltage to a humanly acceptable level and interpreting Divine Revelation in terms of the living of everyday life and the conduct of personal relationships between man and God, and a man and his neighbour.

Theology

Theology seeks to be about God. It is the articulation in human terms of the meaning and implication of mystical experience, of Divine Revelation.

There are, however, many different theologies corresponding to the experiences of different men and women, of different cultures, at different stages in the process of revelation. There are also what are known as theologies which seek to relate the Divine Revelation to specific human issues.

At each stage in the 'stepping down' process the theology becomes more remote from its origins until it finally vanishes into religious philosophy quite unconnected with prayer, or becomes an academic discipline and therefore essentially abstract. Theology is only worthy of the name as long as it retains its mystical connection. Theology is about God, and however admirable its more abstract and academic derivatives may be at their own level, they are not properly called theology unless they are rooted in prayer and prayer is their driving force.

To come to a state of balance in these matters it is necessary to participate deeply in the Mind of Christ. God the Holy Spirit is the best of all theologians and the Divine Grace is the only tutor in the subject. Without total dedication to growth in Grace and full participation in the Mind of Christ, with all that this entails and with all its implications, the theologian will never rise above the level of religious philosopher, for to do theology demands a knowledge of God. This is only possible when the mind is in the heart.

For one who partakes fully in the Mind of Christ, theology is of no further interest, for God IS, and is known and loved, and love determines all things.

Mystical Experience

A mystic is one who is in love with God. The term is misued and misapplied. Mystical experience is a direct experience at the deepest, or highest, level of a man's being of the person-to-person love of God. It is associated, more often than not, with contemplative prayer, but it is not necessarily so associated for it is *given* and cannot be sought.

For a man or a woman to be so confronted is for their whole being to be both integrated and, at the same time, to be thrown into radical disorder. For a sinful human being to be so confronted is a terrible experience, but also a blessed one. With such an experience comes a vocation both to share it and also to interpret it. Neither are possible without both suffering and misunderstanding.

The dilemma of the Church as a whole is the dilemma of the individual. The corporate experience of the Church demands that it be shared, and the sharing is called evangelism. The demand for faithful interpretation results in doctrine. Doctrine and evangelism go hand in hand but neither *are* the experience itself. They seek to draw others into participation in the experience.

The dilemma of the individual is similar to that of the Church as a whole. The experience must be shared, but without drawing attention to the one who has had the experience. It must be interpreted, but this requires years of reflection, informed by the doctrines of the Church as a whole.

Reason and intuition are fully exercised in all this activity and it is by the grace of God that the sharing and the interpretation are faithfully accomplished. God the Holy Spirit is the first evangelist and the surest interpreter of the energies of God as encountered by moral humanity.

Reason and intuition, the two faculties of man by which he is able to know and to understand, must be held together and in balance. In mortal man this is a work of Divine Grace, but without this balance, with each faculty interrogating the other, knowledge will not mature into understanding, and understanding will not mature into wisdom.

Mysticism and theology represent, to some degree, the intuitive and the rational, with the reason articulating what the intuitive side of Man has encountered and perceived. The implications of this encounter, applied to everyday life, issue in morality, and as the revelation is stepped down further it becomes more and more remote from its origins.

The one and the many cannot be separated. A man's or a woman's experience is the experience of Man. The original and ongoing Divine Revelation in Christ is the experience of the Church as a whole and of Christians individually, each according to his or her own needs and nature. The same imperative to share, yet to be self-effacing in sharing, motivates the Church's evangelism and the individual's witness. The same imperative to articulate and rationalise motivates the Church to define her doctrines and individuals to come to terms with their own experiences, aided by the articulated collective wisdom of the Church.

But God is greater than the most faithful doctrines. He is not confined by the restraints men seek to impose upon him for the sake of the tidiness of their own minds. Only a mind which has become a part of the Mind of Christ can discover the wisdom which transcends knowledge and understanding. For such a mind theology and morality are also transcended, for Love alone is its life and motivation.

PART THREE

Men and Women

In the words of St Bernard, Life is only for Love; time is only that we may find God. Mortal life, life on earth, is therefore for the purpose of finding God and being found by God, and in the process learning to love.

Men and women are created to love one another. Each may glimpse God in and through the other. Lovers are granted a vision of the beloved transfigured; and the beauty which is beheld, briefly, is quite other than the beauty which conforms to current criteria of what is attractive or unattractive. In part it is a beauty projected by the beholder, and in part it is a beauty which is revealed to the beholder. And both adoration and worship attend the vision.

The vision does not last, it is fleeting and easily dismissed in later life as belonging to the fancies and follies of youth. Nevertheless the glimpse of the Lover of All in and through the earthly beloved is a theophany, a showing of God, for life is only for love and time is only that we may find God.

A man and a woman are each a Mystery to the other. They will never completely penetrate to a full knowledge of each other. Their mutual understanding will remain limited and there will remain ever more to be discovered, for each completes the other in the process of their own becoming, and each is made whole by the other.

'With my body I thee worship', is an expression of a most profound truth*; for men and women are created by God to

* From the Marriage Rite of the Book of Common Prayer (1662).

worship one another. Worship is the acknowledgement of worth, and each is of infinite worth in the sight of God. Worship is expressed in the total giving of the self and mutual self-giving is the way in which men and women become one, and in the process become fully human.

Man is a threefold being: Spirit, Soul and Body. There must be a meeting between men and women at all these levels. This threefold being, thus described, is of course an oversimplification. The soul cannot be simply identified with psyche or with mind. In some understandings the mind and will are seen as lying behind this threefold model and either seeking the integration of the whole or settling for a lesser good with one or two parts of the whole only.

Men and women arrive at a truthful relationship with each other when the *rapport* between them begins at the level of the Spirit. This encounter at the level of the spirit enables a meeting of minds (souls, psyches) that can be very different indeed but can enrich and complement each other if there is a primary spiritual *rapport*. The body is then able to react and come to its own true *rapport* with the other because the process has started from 'above' and the tone, the character, the integrity, is determined from the higher rather than from the lower.

A relationship which begins from the opposite direction has a much diminished chance of either being or becoming whole, or essentially truthful in respect of the total person of either party. Thus a relationship based primarily on physical attraction can remain at that level, but at some risk of hurt to the total person if it is unable to arrive at a true meeting of minds and a genuine spiritual *rapport*. Thus a man and a woman may discover that they have nothing in common and are indeed tedious to each other on all levels other than the physical. They are fortunate if they are able to emerge from the relationship with no more trauma than an important lesson learned the hard way and nobody seriously damaged.

The model: Spirit, Soul and Body is a useful one provided that it is not overloaded. It indicates priorites, both within a man or a woman and also between a man and a woman. The lower gives expression to the higher. Truth is seldom arrived at from the opposite direction.

Men and women are, all of them, persons of the one being, Man. They are thus members one of another and, in a very real sense, they *are* one another. What happens to any one is happening to Man. The sufferings of Man are suffered by men and women, and the great majority of the sorrows and sufferings of men and women are inflicted upon them by each other, for Man is a fallen creature and all men and women are born in this Original Sin.

The effects of the Fall are twofold: as the integrity of the creature is compromised, security is also compromised. Men and women are fundamentally insecure. And there is a rupture in Man which may best be understood, in terms of the model of Man as a threefold being, as a partial rupture between the spirit on the one hand and soul and body on the other. This is, of course, an oversimplification but it will serve to aid understanding so long as it is recognized as such.

The relationships between men and women are put at hazard by the fact that neither party is integrated and both are sinners. In each, the ego is enthroned as a god and there is a conformity with the criteria of the lesser good. Where ego is god, all other egos are a threat and so other persons are reduced to the level, either of 'things', or of sub-persons who may or may not be desired by the ego for its own satisfaction. Men and women therefore want each other for motives that are mixed. Affection is untempered by respect, and it is easy for appetite to get the upper hand.

This state of affairs is, in part, the lot of every mortal man and woman. Its manifestations vary with individuals, but truth and wholeness in persons and in their relationships is, in the natural order, perpetually subject to compromise. By the Grace of God, men and women may be brought into the Way of Integration and Perfection. The closer either comes to the Mind of Christ, the more fulfilling are their relationships likely to be and the deeper their joy in each other; for life is only for love, and time is only that we may find God.

Original Sin has caused man to invest his relationships with a terrible solemnity. Men and women, whose relationships at any and every level are designed by God to be of the very essence of joy, are imprisoned in a spider's web of inhibition, shame, uncertainty, guilt and humourless legalism. Even the ridiculous, which is part of the joy, is turned into ridicule which is bitter and destructive.

This is a partial state, but all men and women partake of it. Integration and joy are part and parcel of each other. The body is a cheerful animal, innocent as a child. The spirit is filled with a childlike sense of fun. The mind, dominated by the ego and only fitfully in touch with the spirit, hides from its insecurities in excesses, either of prudishness or obscenity. The natural and blessed physical encounter between man and woman is either identified with sin and feared, or it is made the subject of obsession in the opposite direction. In either event, joy is banished and the wholeness of humanity is inhibited and denied.

Men and women are intended by God to enjoy one another. Joy is only possible in the context of truthfulness, affection and respect. The absurdities, the fun, joy itself, depend upon security and integrity. In an integrated man or woman, the spirit finds physical expression in and through the body. There is no fear, no insecurity. That which is uniquely appropriate is given expression with neither inhibition nor excess. The motivation is self-forgetting and there are no threats. Law is transcended because Love knows instinctively what is appropriate. It is the partial disintegration within Man which has partially disintegrated the relationship between men and women, all of whom are sinners.

The Mind of Christ knows no fear, no inhibition, no obsession, no prudishness. It is full of fun, enjoys the ridiculous to the full, and its infinite compassion and affection are matched by an infinite respect for each and every creature. Spirit, soul and body are at one in the fullness of self-giving joy.

Men and women are different and they complement each other. This difference and this mutually complementary nature extends throughout their total being. The spirits of men and women are not the same, neither are their minds, or their bodies. Each, while complete, completes the other and is raised to a new and other wholeness by the other, and this at every level.

The body gives expression to the truth of the total relationship. This it does by expressing affection and respect, comfort, tenderness and compassion in very many ways with a nearly infinite degree of subtlety of nuance, appropriate to the persons, the relationship and the circumstances. When the body is giving expression to the spirit, all is well and all is appropriate, for the mind is in the heart and the Mind of Christ is engaged in the relationship. The bodies, being different, will proclaim and celebrate their difference and differences. They will celebrate and express the truth of separateness, and they will celebrate and express the truth of union. And the celebration of truth is blessed.

Sinful men and women are hard put to it to know the truth, and harder pressed still to maintain it. When the body is giving expression to the mind only, then it is in danger of being put into one false position after another, for the mind and the corrupted will of man find truth in relationships hard to find or to handle. The lesser good tends always to prevail and what is designed as self-giving is misused in exploitation. The ego seeks to be god and demands satisfaction of its desires and appetites. Love seeks to give self in restraint and respect; lust seeks to exploit for self-satisfaction and has to be restrained by law, which is as ineffectual as it is usually corrupt.

So joy gives place to fear; fun gives place to fascination; confidence gives place to radical insecurity and mistrust, and nobody really knows what to do for spending all their time thinking about it!

107

Love

Men and women are the greatest potential means of Grace to each other. They complement each other, so long as self-forgetting love is the motivation behind their relationship, whatever that relationship may be. Their ministry to each other is one of encouragement and fulfilment, each seeking the emergence of the whole person and the realisation of the whole potential of that person. Concern for the other and forgetfulness of self will accomplish the same in the self.

Love knows no threats. Men and women threaten each other at any level only because of insecurity. The insecure will seek to inhibit the other, to prevent his or her becoming, lest that becoming be a bigger threat. Where ego reigns supreme there is no true ministry to another, for all is subordinated to the ego and the realisation of the potential of another is only tolerable if it can be used to bolster the ego. Thus for example, an ambitious wife will goad her husband on to attain some position of eminence in order that she herself may be important in society. An insecure husband will seek to inhibit his wife's fulfilment lest she outgrow him and diminish him further.

Love knows no such threats. The fulfilment of one is the joy of the other. The withholding of the possibilities of fulfilment from the other is both a hurt to the other and a hurt to the self. For men and women are members one of another, and they project upon each other the disorders within, and are themselves diminished by the act of projection.

Men and women are to see God in each other, to approach each other with awe and in tenderness, for each represents to the other a facet of the unknowable mystery of Man, behind which is always the unknowable Mystery of God.

Procreation

The bringing of children into the world is the supreme act of creation that man achieves. And it is Man in Man's wholeness that is involved, as men and women together and in union conceive the child.

The act of union, in Man, has become separated from the conception of children in that it is relatively easy to prevent conception taking place. This is an example of man's inventiveness and creativity and it cannot be un-invented any more than the atomic bomb can be un-invented. Men and women are obliged to come to terms with the possible implications for the structures and stability of society. There are consequences built in to all the creations of mankind and one as profound as this is certainly no exception.

Children require a stable, loving home, and the wholeness of a man and a woman in caring for them if they are to reach their own adulthood in wholeness and without trauma. This is an unchanging need. The lifelong union of a man and a woman is the true context for the birth and upbringing of children. But all men and all women are sinners, and the world abounds with catastrophe, so this ideal state of affairs is not always achieved or maintained.

The act of union, before it was able to be separated from the conception of children, rightfully belonged to the lifelong union of man and woman, if only for the sake of the children. It expressed and celebrated lifelong union; the total gift of either to other in creative co-operation with Almighty God. This it still does, supremely, in the holy estate of matrimony.

The body must express the truth. A relationship between a man and a woman has a physical expression of some kind, and the truth will be found when the minds of both parties are in their hearts. Love rather than law determines this, for law does not always keep up with

the changing problems that human creativity presents. Love alone is the criterion; but all men and women are sinners.

Integrity

'Am I my brother's keeper?' asked Cain, having murdered his brother Abel. Every person of the being, man, is his or her brother's keeper, and his or her sister's keeper, for we are all members one of another and our integrity is bound up with each other.

Men and women are responsible for each other and they are responsible to each other. Wilful irresponsibility is sin by definition, for it is a denial of humanity. The integrity of a woman must be sacred to a man. The integrity of a man must be sacred to a woman. It is not possible to play fast and loose with the integrity of another without losing one's own, and this at every level of a person's being.

The relationship between any man and any woman has its own integrity, and the physical expression of that relationship must maintain that integrity. The maintenance of its integrity is as likely to be put at risk by untruthful restraint as by untruthful excess, for truth requires to be expressed at every level.

Men and women have a ministry to one another to make each other whole, to care selflessly for the total person of the other. It is not possible to write a book of rules to regulate every possible relationship between every possible man and woman, for each one is unique and each has its own character and integrity. And each relationship is itself in relationship with a multitude of other relationships, involving one or both parties. The integrity of them all must be regarded as sacred, and maintained accordingly.

None of this is possible for sinful men and women, unaided by Divine Grace. But with God, all things are possible. Men and women are all sinners; all make mistakes, all fall short in one way or another. Christ alone is their integrity and they abide in an ambience of perpetual forgiveness and restoration. It is better to err by loving too much than to err by loving too little!

Men and women together make up Man, the creature. This is the primary fact of mortal life. In heaven, as Scripture teaches us, other conditions apply, but the love of men and women for each other is taken up on to another plane altogether. Nothing is lost; all is fulfilled.

Traditionally, among many Christians, marriage following a bereavement was regarded as savouring somewhat of adultery, for the relationship made on earth was projected into heaven in very earthly terms. Relationships as fundamental as a fulfilled and blessed marriage do indeed extend into heaven, but heaven is not exclusive. Heaven is all-embracing in its Love. What is impossible on earth is fulfilled in heaven. In mortal life, only one who is secure within a truly blessed marriage is secure enough to relate to others of the opposite sex with the totality of his or her being without threat to one party or another. Earthly life demands an exclusive relationship in order that others may be included without threats or loss of integrity. Heaven is quite different, for all threats have vanished and integrity is secure. And men and women neither marry nor are given in marriage, for they are as the angels.

Men and women do not relate to each other according to a book of rules or even a moral code. These are man-made and seek to safeguard society against the excesses of sinners, and all are sinners. They are remote interpretations, at many removes, of the Revelation of God to man, but they inevitably fail to some degree in that they are dealing with flesh and blood, and they are dealing with images of God. And every one is unique. Laws and moral codes are guidelines, and frequently excellent as such, but they are neither life nor love itself.

111

An awe and a respect for the integrity of the other, and a respect for the integrity of all other persons and relationships will guide men and women into the truth. For their relationships are of the heart, and if their minds are in their hearts, all will be well with their relationships.

Man's encounter with God in prayer has drawn from him words which belong to the love-affairs of men and women in order to articulate the relationship of which he has discovered himself to be a part. Holy Matrimony signifies to us 'the mystical union that is betwixt Christ and his Church'*. The Church collectively is the Bride of Christ, and also the Body of Christ by virtue of the union between them. Nuptial imagery alone seems able to do justice to the heights of the mystical experience of Man.

The love of men and women for each other is therefore understood as deriving from the Love of God for Man, the Love of Christ for His Church, the love of the Creator for creatures. It is a holy mystery, and by it Man becomes one within himself. The polarity of earthly creation, summed up in men and women, is made articulate and in them, and the love each has for the other, the union of heaven and earth is symbolised, celebrated and effected.

Man is God's priest to earthly creation. The love of men and women for each other is the sacrificial offering of earthly life and its polarities to the Creator who is Love and the source of all life and love.

A man and a woman are priest and priestess. Together they perform the priesthood of Man. Together they manage the world they inhabit and together they exercise the stewardship over God's creatures which was bestowed upon them in their creation. It is man and woman together that is the image of God, for together they constitute Man.

---

* The form of Solemnization of Matrimony in the Book of Common Prayer, 1662.

Worship

Worship is the expression of worth. The worth that is expressed is the worth of Man in the sight of God, for Man cannot in any way contemplate a 'worth' for God. Worship is a celebration of Love. It is an act of Love, a self-giving. The corporate worship of Christians is a celebration of their relationship with God in and through the humanity of Christ. That relationship is best expressed in nuptial imagery, for the Church is the Bride of Christ and, as such, His Body for she is 'one flesh' with Him.

Of all the ways in which Christians worship, one only is commanded in Holy Scripture by the Lord Himself. Christians are to make Eucharist. The Church meets on the first day of the week, the weekly Easter, to celebrate and proclaim the death and the Resurrection of Christ in the offering of the bread and the wine, and in their reception as the Body and the Blood of Christ. In respect of this simple act a lifetime of meditations will not suffice; its richness is inexhaustible, but it is in the making of Eucharist that the gathered Christian people *become* the Church. Christ Himself presides at his mysteries; time is taken up into timelessness and the whole Church, in heaven and on earth, is at one in this act of union which is both once and for all and also perpetual while time lasts.

As the act of union between man and woman is the supreme, creative act of Love and self-giving, so the Eucharist is the act of union between Christ and His Church. It is the supreme creative and redemptive act of love and self-giving for it is wholly one with the self-giving death of Christ on the Cross – the consummation of the union of God and Man – and with that perpetual altar in heaven where stands the Lamb of God, 'slain from the foundation of the world'. All other acts of worship, private and corporate, are taken up into the Eucharistic offering, and the whole life of the Christian Church on earth flows from its altars and returns to them in perpetual self-offering.

Worship is Man's expression of love, awe, and dependency upon 'That which is Wholly Other'. It is, in part, addressed to a man's own self in that it is a reminder of reality and an acknowledgement of truth. Worship is an emptying out before God. It predisposes a man's mind to find his heart and there encounter God the Holy Spirit. Worship is thus both objective and subjective, and it is addressed to God alone.

A man will inevitably begin to resemble the object of his worship. He will become in part possessed by it. It therefore matters exceedingly that he worships in truth, and worships God as He is revealed in truth rather than man-made idols projected between man and the truth.

Worship makes a man. Worship is central to humanity itself. There are two possible objects of worship. One is God, the other is the ego. Fallen man is a past-master at self-deception and therefore all his worship is, to a degree, syncretistic. He worships God, and at the same time worships his own ego via God! The detection of this error is never easy and it is a lifelong task to eradicate it, aided by Divine Grace. A man may deceive himself, he is less likely to deceive his fellow men and women and he cannot deceive God. Truth will out. Only reality is real.

Worship is conducted at many levels. Beneath the worship due to God alone is another level of worship. It is due by a man to a woman, and by a woman to a man. Each is, for the other, an icon of God. Each is a sacramental presence for the other. But both are sinners.

Worship is the expression of worth: Man's worth in the

sight of God and, on a lower level, the worth of man and woman in each other's sight and in the sight of God who is encountered in their love for one another.

Prayer

The prayers that men and women offer to God are addressed to themselves! They are an articulation of a mixture of belief and desire. The Collects of the Day in, for example, the Book of Common Prayer, are masterpieces in this respect and many of them give the impression of having been compiled with great precision by a lawyer. They state Man's belief in the nature of God as revealed in Jesus Christ and extend that belief into a petition which is very clearly stated, and offered to the Father through – that is to say by virtue of – Jesus Christ the incarnate Son of God, through whose humanity a human relationship with God is possible.

Prayer is not merely a man talking to himself. Prayer proceeds from deeper levels altogether and the words of a spoken prayer are very much the 'surface level' of the prayer, reminding the man what the prayer is about rather than informing the Almighty.

The Eucharistic Prayers of the Church illustrate this admirably. They seek to give expression to the faith of the Church in its wholeness. They are a Creed. The words are addressed to the Church and remind the Church on earth of its faith. They rehearse the mighty acts of God in creation and redemption. They proclaim unity with the Church in heaven. They make intercession for the Church on earth and with the Eucharistic action they recall and invoke the Saving Mysteries of Christ into the present moment and unite time with timelessness. The words proclaim the faith of the Church. God needs no reminders; man does!

In the Eucharist therefore, the Church as a whole stands before God with her mind in her heart. Her collective mind articulates her faith and proclaims God's Love, and she offers herself in and with the Eucharistic action.

The words of any prayer are, as it were, the musical accompaniment to the song which is sung by the heart. When the words are faithful and true they enter the heart and become part of the silence of heaven.

Worship involves the totality of a man's or a woman's being. Spirit, mind and body are all involved, each giving expression to the self-offering of the total person. Thus posture, gesture and the dance are all involved in worship. Ritual and formality come naturally to worship. The postures of Hatha-Yoga are profoundly worshipful and are designed to prepare, and to aid the total person to worship through meditation and, if prayer to God is the intention, to contemplation.

Christians are released from the idea of the sacred posture. Any posture is sacred if it is the posture in which prayer is made. The body gives expression to the mind and to the spirit in worship, and the postures it adopts are those which express the relationship between God and man. These vary according to the understanding which is current. Thus in the Christian West, kneeling expresses the relationship between subject and king. In the Christian East, men and women stand before God, for they are found worthy in Christ to stand before Him, and kneeling is therefore inappropriate.

In the mutual worship of man and woman, posture, gesture and the dance are so fundamental as to be unconscious to the participants. The body speaks its own language, pays its own court. Words fail, but the silent communications of the spirit and the postures, gestures and dances of the body communicate at a depth beyond the reach of language.

The liturgical worship of the Church is easily rendered formal and stilted by the penning of bodies into pews or into lines of uncomfortable chairs. Spontaneity is destroyed. Too frequently, kneeling is an agony, standing a hardship and sitting recollectedly a difficulty. When the body is thus trapped, worship retreats to the head and becomes mind-centred. Mind-centred worship tends always in the direction of sentimentality. Christians must be reminded that they meet for worship as lovers of God, and that the spontaneous worship of the body expresses the worship of the spirit and keeps the mind in its proper place.

Worship comes from the heart. There is a measure of formality about it, for the body will make its own forms of expression, but worship *as a formality* is no worship at all and is better not perpetrated.

The body, left to its own devices and uninhibited by the mind's inhibitions, will naturally give expression to the heart. But the heart is paramount; here is the seat of love, here God is encountered. A congregation met together at the altar of God is physically orientated on the altar, but the encounter in the heart of the worshipper takes place in the heart and not outside it. The external, 'beyond myself' concentration and the desire to give self to 'That which is other than me', opens the doors within to an encounter in the depths of the being.

Worship is the conduct of a fervent love-affair. It is said of mystics that they are in love with God. The state of being in love with God is what worship is all about. There is a difference between loving another and being in love with another. The former state is self-forgetful and detached, being concerned for the total wellbeing of the other. The latter state is one of desperate desire for identification with the beloved. It desires to give self to the beloved and to have the beloved for itself. Being in love is a necessary preliminary to loving in full maturity.

It is appropriate to Man's mortal life that he be in love with God. Mortal life is a state of immaturity and it is appropriate that the lover should seek to give himself to the Beloved and seek the Beloved for his very own. This is worship on earth. Worship in heaven is more nearly the mutual indwelling of

117

the long-time happily married, whose identification with each other is secure and whose love is self-forgetting and detached.

It has been said that it is impossible to speak of God without passion. It is a sadness that so many Christians think it necessary to try!

Liturgy

Worship is both an individual and a corporate activity. Corporate worship can easily become formal and institution-alised. If conducted without imagination or sensitivity it can do much to inhibit, if not to stultify, the stirrings towards worship of those gathered together. The conduct of worship is therefore something of an art.

Liturgical worship must be so familiar to those taking part that they are able to make responses and join together in corporate prayers almost without thinking. The mind must be in the heart if worship is to be true and fulfilled. The mind cannot be in the heart if it is required to abide in the head, looking up unfamiliar and too often changing words. There is a tradition in the Christian East that worshippers should not have books in their hands during the Liturgy because their prayer will be inhibited thereby. Prayer comes from the heart. The words of the Liturgy are, in large measure, a kind of corporate mantram. They have their meaning, but the real worship is beyond words and at a depth far deeper than the mere meaning of words.

Liturgy is poetry and the dance. It must lift the worship-pers to a new level and enable them to join with each other in charity. They must come to a common mind, both conscious and unconscious. The part played by those leading the worship is important, for their recollection, their own encounter within, will convey itself to those participating and add a needed dimension to the functions they objectively perform. Worship is both objective and subjective and the bringing of all participants into true worship at the Liturgy is an art, and more than an art. It is a grace for which those whose responsibility it is must pray.

Liturgy is a courtly dance and a formal act, corporately offered. It is objective worship, but it comes to its true fulfilment when love and the desire to give the self to the Beloved is fully roused in all participating.

Worship is motivated by a deep desire for fulfilment. There is what has been described as a 'God-shaped hole' in Man and he is restless until it is filled and he is made whole in the process. A deep longing for God is a vocation given to many. The vocation is, in a sense, the gift of awareness of the God-shaped hole within them and their motivation is the motivation of a lover who is separated from his beloved and can only gaze from the garden at the window behind which the beloved is concealed. There is an anguish, a forlornness, which is at the heart of what is a blessed vocation.

Sometimes this God-shaped hole is filled in part by an earthly partner in whom, and through whom, the lover sees God. The earthly partner is a blessed sacrament of the ultimate Lover, the ultimate Beloved. The underlying longing still remains, but on a different level. The vocation is fulfilled by this means, each partner being a means of grace to the other.

Sometimes the longing for God altogether transcends the most blessed earthly partnership and becomes the perceived reality of mortal life. This is a hard vocation to bear but it is a blessed one. It may find expression in hermitage, cloister or market-place; in celebacy or in the married state. These are but means of expressing the truth of the vocation as it is known and lived by the individual. Those blessed with such a vocation carry on behalf of others the sharp awareness of the God-shaped hole in man of which multitudes are unaware and uncaring. The few suffer for the many, but it is a blessed suffering.

The vocation of man is not to worship, but *to be worship*. Those whose vocation it is to be filled with an insatiable longing for God are called to be what man must become. They are unprofitable servants, for they are only doing what it is their duty to do.

Worship is a formal observance. It is an act of will in order that sinful man may be recalled to realities. The loving Providence of God must be totally relied upon but never taken for granted. Love takes nothing for granted, for to take another person for granted is to display ego-worship at the heart of a love-affair.

Worship is therefore a formal and freely-willed acknowledgement of God's Love and a deliberate offering of self. It transcends the whims and fancies of the moment. It takes no account of the subjective and ego-centred feelings. Worship is owed to the loved one as a due, and its offering rekindles love in the fickle heart of man.

Courtesy and what are known as good manners are a formal acknowledgement of the respect due to another as a person beloved of God. Discourtesy and bad manners are the most vivid manifestation of ego-worship and are offensive to experience and to behold because they betray an idolatry which denies humanity to all except the perpetrator's ego.

Courtesy and good manners are due to Almighty God. They are paid in formal worship and in its reverend offering. This is a recalling of the worshippers to a sense of the relationship between Creator and creature. The formal prayers of the Liturgy are the formalities of good manners. The careful phraseology, seeking to proclaim the Church's faith in its wholeness, and acknowledging the Love of God in all its manifestations, are a courtesy. The training of a child in good manners – and in the reasons for it – disciplines an ever-demanding ego and makes the child mindful of the dignity of others. All mortal men and women are the children of God and require to be similarly trained for very similar reasons, but on a higher level.

'He who loves me will keep my commandments'. There is an obvious test of the truth of any man's or woman's devotion to the Lord. They either seek to do what he says or they do not. The ego strives with the Almighty, the lesser good clamours for acceptance. The one and the many manifest their devotion in similar ways.

The Incarnate Son of God left to His Church but one new Commandment: Love one another. He left but one act of distinctively Christian worship: the Eucharist. The two are inseparable, for to meet together to offer the Eucharist presupposes that those meeting are at peace with one another. It is impossible to meet at the altar to invoke the Saving Mysteries of Christ and to make the act of self-offering in union with the self-offering of Christ on the Cross, and be radically out of charity with the other participants. The Church has always warned her members of the need to be in a state of Grace before presuming to receive the Blessed Sacrament of the Body and Blood of Christ.

Christian worship is corporate. It is the corporate offering of those who are at peace with one another, taken up into the Love-Affair of the Everblessed Trinity. It is by their Love for one another that Christians are recognizable. If they are unrecognizable the reason is plain. But all are sinners.

The Eucharist is of our Lord's own institution. He is celebrant at every altar; He is victim and He is priest. His Church is caught up into, and identified with, His mysteries and His own self. It is the Eucharist that causes an assembly of Christians to be the Church. At the altar of God none are excluded save those who exclude themselves.

To worship is to stand before God with the mind in the heart. When all else is said and done, this alone is left. The encounter with God takes place in the heart. It is in the timeless centre of a man or woman, that indefinable part that we identify with the heart, that God the Holy Spirit dwells. It is there that all commerce between the various levels of a man's own being takes place, and it is there that all communication between the worlds is effected in truth.

What is true for the one is true for the corporate whole. Liturgical worship, and pre-eminently the Eucharist, is a corporate standing before God with the mind in the heart. It is an exercise in the timeless and an invocation of the Eternal. The commerce between the worlds takes place at the altar of God which is the heart of the Church. The Lord of the Dance is the celebrant and the Great Dance of Creation is the Liturgy of the totality of creatures throughout all ages, in which they return to him who gave them their being and go forth with that being renewed. The Eucharist is a summing up of the Great Dance, and Man partakes of the office and ministry of the Great High Priest, who has identified fallen and sinful Man with himself.

To worship is to exist. Worship is the fulfilment of man's being; it is the giving of self to the Giver of All Selves. It is the act of self-giving love. Worship makes the worshipper; the Eucharist makes the Church. Between men and women, their mutual worship causes each one to become something other than would otherwise be possible, for their relationship signifies something greater than itself: the mystical union betwext Christ and His Church, the eternal Love-Affair which, so far as man's understanding can reach, is the very nature of the Everblessed Trinity.

Heaven

The idea of a three-tier universe dies hard. As a model it has its uses, but an understanding of heaven as the first floor of a building, with hell in the basement and everything that matters going on at ground-floor level, has haunted the imagination of mortal man for centuries, if not for millennia. And being haunted is a morbid experience.

Heaven is better understood as a state of normality and of unimpeded becoming. Heaven begins, or at least is able to begin, in the mortal life of a man or a woman. Heaven is a state of Grace, and the Divine Grace operates in men and women in mortal life in so far as they seek it and permit it. Heaven is decidedly the will of God for all creatures, and Christians believe that the Incarnation of the Son of God was for the purpose of bringing fallen man into the way of normality, the way of unimpeded becoming that we know by the name of heaven.

Images of celestial idleness, with or without harps, are inappropriate to the point of mischief. The use, on tombstones, of such words as 'resting' or 'sleeping' is unfortunate if not actually unfaithful. To rest in the Lord is not to put one's feet on a heavenly mantlepiece in supine content. It is to *abide* in unimpeded trust and confidence in the Everlasting Love. The 'sleeping' referred to in memorials is conducted with an extraordinary vigour!

Heaven is a state of mind, and the Mind is that of Christ. By the Divine Grace, mortal men and women are able to grow towards, and into, a participation in that Mind. This growth, begun in earthly life, continues in that continuum in which men and women find themselves when earthly life has been left behind. The whole business of growth into the Mind of Christ is what heaven is all about, and this concentrates a man's attention, not on an imagined hereafter, but in the *present moment*, be it on earth or after earthly life. For as Christians have often been reminded, it is in their present moments that men and women are able to relate to Almighty God.

Heaven is a state of affairs within which an infinite number of worlds, dimensions and planes of being abide. The earth itself abides in heaven but man does not. The heavenly dimensions of the earth will be revealed to man at the Second Coming, but of these mysteries it is better not to speculate.

Heaven is therefore very far from being an exclusive club for the righteous on the top floor of the skyscraper of creation. Within the broad definition of heaven there are, as Jesus put it, 'many rooms'. The process of becoming, begun in mortal life by Divine Grace, continues eternally, for to cease to grow and to change is to cease to exist. There are many men and women in mortal life who exhibit all the appearances of earthly living but whose hold on existence is tenuous in the extreme. Jesus, in His earthly ministry, warned of *Gehanna*, the rubbish dump. Consignment to this end is self-chosen entirely, but the free will of men and women is sacred to God. Eternal Love will not dehumanise a man or a woman by depriving them of their free will, and the ambience of forgiveness in which all mankind abides is capable of being rejected, for Love is vulnerable and Eternal Love is absolutely vulnerable.

Heaven is not a single state, plane, dimension or world. It is not a static condition but a living dynamic. It may not be imagined by projecting the time–space continuum of earthly life into an imaginary dimension decked out with pious trappings. It is better to believe than to speculate, but it is not unreasonable for mortal man to expect some kind of continuum, some points of reference by which he may know himself to exist and recognize the existence of others.

Heaven is a state of mind, the Mind of Christ. For one who is beginning to participate in that Mind, however fleetingly, the matter of earthly death assumes a diminished importance as the whole of mortality is transcended and the whole being is in slow process of transfiguration. Eternal Life knows no absolute parameters; it is all-embracing and all things in heaven and earth are its concern.

Perfection is a *way*; that is to say that it is a dynamic process and not a static state. The way of perfection is beginningless and endless; it follows that an image of heaven as a state of total perfection arrived at immediately *post-mortem* is naive to say the very least. By the same token, a similar image of hell as a static state of perpetual, mechanical torment, reserved for those who have not fulfilled the appropriate criteria in earthly life is equally naive.

The *post-mortem* state is not to be arbitrarily identified either with heaven or with hell. It may be either, or neither. It may be closely earthbound and wordly in its concerns. It is better not to speculate in detail, and doctrines of Purgatory are only helpful in that they suggest that the way of perfection, begun in this life by Divine Grace, continues hereafter and is dynamic rather than static.

To depart this life is not to be awarded an immediate doctorate in celestial divinity. Ignorance survives the tomb, and knowledge, understanding and wisdom are slow in their development in any continuum in which fallen and redeemed men and women may find themselves. The criteria are few and simple: Faith and Love. The examiner is a man's or a woman's own heart when confronted with reality. This can take place before or after death and it is a confrontation which is ongoing. The Love of God determines at what stage it shall take place; the Everlasting Love is the master of all timing, both in time and in timelessness.

Death must not be taken too lightly, for it is a moment of truth, a time of change which is fundamental. It must be approached in a faithful agnosticism. This means that it is better not to fill the head with man-made images about the

125

hereafter but to wait and see how gracious the Lord is. But death must not be taken too seriously either. It is the gateway to a Great Adventure, a shedding of the burdens of physical ageing and limitation in this life and, if approached in faith, hope and love, the doorway through to the Beloved.

Heaven is the realm of God and of His Holy Angels. All things are in God and all is heaven, save that which has lost its integrity. Heaven, for men and for women, is a growth process, a realisation of an integrity not only restored but recreated. Human life, in Christ, is lived according to a wholly new contract for existence.

Heaven is the realm of God and of His Holy Angels. The services of angels and men are constituted in a wonderful order, as the Michaelmas collect proclaims, and the two quite different orders of being complement each other in a way mortal man cannot ever comprehend, even though at times he may be in various ways conscious of their presence and ministry.

Heaven is a state of mind, the Mind of Christ. The angelic order impinges upon the human, both in heaven and on earth. But among mortal men and women there is not the state of mind to acknowledge the fact. The natural response of fallen man to something that is other than his own order of being is either to arbitrarily deny its existence or to seek to turn it to his own ends. Man's own ends are notorious: personal and group profit and power. Mortal man would seek a military use of the angelic order against his own kind if he had the slightest regular inkling of its presence!

Jesus is recorded, in the Fourth Gospel, as using the Greek idea of *cosmos*, i.e. order in an orderly world, to mean *chaos*, its opposite. It is a grim humour but a stark realism. The world, *cosmos*, the world that is of human values, is chaotic. It is *chaos*, thinly papered over. The 'peace' of fallen Man is an armed truce with seething hatreds and disorder just

126

beneath the surface. Nothing works. There is no worldly remedy for the world. The world, regarded by mortal men and women as normality, is in fact the utterly abnormal from whose chaos and malignancy man is redeemed in Christ. The normal is not the world, nor even the beautiful earth that fallen man inhabits. The normal, the real, is heaven; the realm of God, His Holy Angels, and men and women deified.

Any attempt to define the progress of the human soul *post-mortem* is doomed to failure. Doctrines of Purgatory or of Paradise can do no more than indicate states of being which are transitory and not to be thought of either as heaven or as hell. They proclaim the Love of God for sinners, and the will of God that sinners should not perish but have Eternal Life.

The *post-mortem* states from which psychically perceived communications are claimed very frequently offer evidence of an exceedingly worldly-minded triviality. The more eager the communicator, the more trivial the communication. From another level can come, on occasion, esoteric teachings of a kind which has echoes and parallels in many cultures and which can display considerable awareness of the mechanics of the human system, together with a surprising ignorance of religious concerns. A picture, built up from such material, suggests a number of earthbound, earth-orientated, transitory states inhabited by human souls at a very wide spectrum of *becoming* on many levels. Perhaps this should not surprise us; nor should the still very worldly concerns and behaviour occasionally met with.

This whole area is not what we mean by heaven. The operations of Divine Grace within it are not our concern, and the possibilities of subjective delusion and both simple, and not-so-simple error are considerable. The psychic sensitivities on the natural level can at best encounter what is of nature rather than what is of nature transfigured by grace. The faculty of discernment is uncertain, and it is by grace only that that which is objectively evil can be discerned for what it is. The psychic faculties are to be affirmed and by no means denied, but it is only by the Divine Grace that they can be transfigured and, with the mind in the heart, encounter heaven.

The encounters with heaven that are, from time to time, given to mortal men and women are of a character so wholly other than the shadowy and uncertain communications on the psychic level as to be unmistakable. They are characterised by compassion, light and radiant good humour. They are vital, and there is not the remotest hint of morbidity about them.

Heaven breaks in upon mortal consciousness when love deems it appropriate. The initiatives come from the common Mind of Christ and do not necessarily conform to expected criteria, or even to worldly ideas of good taste! Heaven does not think as the world thinks, and reveals itself how and to whom it chooses, for love's sake.

Thus the Holy Mother of God, and those known by the Church as Saints, are encountered by very ordinary people in very ordinary circumstances. Sometimes there is a great work to be undertaken, as at Lourdes. More often the ministry is to the individual, who seldom talks of it save to a very few who are able to be told. Pearls are not cast before swine, as our Lord reminds us.

The Holy Angels are also encountered from time to time, as their ministry is appropriate to those to whom it is given. The intuitive faculty in mortal men and women is engaged, and phenomena not infrequently accompany the visitations of heaven. But phenomena are not important, and what is important is quite obvious and beyond all argument or question to those in receipt of heaven's direct visitations.

The transcending of the boundaries of heaven and earth is not exclusive to the Mother of God, the Saints and the Holy Angels. Very ordinary men and women sometimes do the same, but the details of their visitations are usually shared only in confidence by those who have known, thereby, that the Mind of Christ has but one motivation: the Everlasting Love of God for sinful men and women.

The Church

The life of the Church on earth is eucharistic, that is to say that it is a life of thanksgiving. The Church lives her life in the context of the Death and Resurrection of Christ as proclaimed in her worship. Her altars invoke the Saving Mysteries in which she abides in perfect thanksgiving.

The life and worship of the Church on earth is not confined to the Church on earth. Heaven is all about, and the Eucharist is the point of meeting between the Church in heaven and the Church on earth. Heaven permeates the whole life of the earthly Church which would otherwise sink into triviality and ecclesiastical politics of the worst sort. It is heaven that maintains the Church on earth and rescues her from her in-built follies; not once, not twice, but perpetually.

The Church on earth has a horizontal cast of mind, she finds it hard to lift her eyes, and the crowing of cocks on an ecclesiastical dung-hill drowns her inner voice, particularly in the context of her hierarchies and those aspiring, in worldly fashion, to high office. It is the vested interest of clerics that maintains the divisions of the Church on earth. She looks back often and forward seldom. She cannot see that, in the light of the unbreakable union between the Church on earth and the Church in heaven, the divisions of the Church on earth are an absurdity and utterly unreal.

The Church on earth does not trust heaven because she cannot control it. Heaven must be regulated lest it becomes excessive and makes the Faithful untidy! Heaven must be denied, or near-denied, if the conceit of the clever is to be maintained. But heaven continues to be heaven, and rescues the earthly Church from her follies perpetually. The Mind of Christ thinks differently from the theological politics of earthly hierarchs and the worldly religiosity of so many of the faithful as they all seek, by Divine Grace, to grow towards and into that same Mind. The Church on earth, empowered to absolve in God's Name, abides herself in an ambience of perpetual absolution. It is just as well!

Heaven is the realm of God and of His Holy Angels. Hell, in poetic terms, is the realm of the devil and his angels. But it is a dolorous poetry and in so far as it may suggest a kind of dualism, a rivalry between Good and Evil, each with his armies, it is unsatisfactory and unfaithful because false.

The dolorous mystery of objective evil is beyond mortal man's understanding. He experiences it, his life is radically affected by it both directly and indirectly, and he is vulnerable to its subtle blandishments; but of its nature and the reason why it is permitted he must remain ignorant and questioning.

It is enough to take note of the poetry of the Holy Scriptures. Evil is personalised, and very specifically by Jesus. The suggestion is of an angelic fall from Grace of some kind, taking man with it. The 'prince of this world' is cast out in the Ministry of God Incarnate; Man is released from a thraldom but is still embattled until the Second Coming. Man's present experience of objective evil is therefore suggested as temporary.

It is suggested by some that the evil one is in the state of 'having been an archangel'. The matter can be left there. Speculation is inappropriate and it is a morbid activity to give energy to dolours of this kind. Mortal men and women are better occupied in bringing to mind the image of *Gehenna*, the rubbish dump, that Jesus uttered uninhibited warnings about. The possibility is presented of a state of 'having been a human being' and it is one most decidedly to be avoided!

Heaven is the realm of just men made perfect. No men or women are just and none are perfect, for all are sinners. But heaven is the realm of those who are committed to the way of perfection in their hearts, and maintained in the way by Divine Grace.

Men and women who seek heaven must expect heaven. Seek and ye shall find, said Jesus. But what a man seeks, he finds, and so it is as well to seek wisely. The heart is the seeker, but the mind must be in the heart if heaven is to be found. Men and women must set their sights firmly on heaven. To aim for a lower mark is to find it. The choice is the individual's very own. The heart's true priorities will determine what is found. Men and women get what they truly seek, but not all want it when they have it. Man is a sinner, and God loves man with an Everlasting Love. Men and women have to learn to know what to seek; the provisions for learning *post-mortem* can only be a matter of speculation, and the matter is best left in the loving hands of God.

Men and women who seek heaven must expect heaven. There is no human qualification other than the tenor of a life motivated from within and open to Divine Grace. There is no innate quality in man that should qualify him for a place 'on high'. Man is a sinner through and through and has no worth of his own and no 'righteousness' whatsoever. He is able to aspire to the realm of God and His Holy Angels because the Word became flesh and dwelt among us, and for no other reason whatsoever.

A man must set his sights on heaven. If instead he sets his sights on being a hierarch in an earth-bound limbo of impeccable respectability, he may get his desire. He may yet be rescued from it, but that is a matter beyond our present concerns.

131

Man is a thought in the Mind of God. Men and women are all persons of the one being, Man. The persons are spread throughout heaven, they are to be found in mortal life on earth, and they inhabit states of being which are, to use a useful term 'transitional'. Man is therefore partially in heaven. All the persons of the being, Man, are members one of another. Within any person, all the levels may be found, in principle at least. What happens to any one is happening to Man. What happens to Man is happening to every man and woman in heaven, on earth, and otherwise situated.

It is necessary for mortal men and women to remember of whom they are persons. Men and women are not windowless monads, nor can they be separated from one another. Jean-Paul Sartre, a playwright, made one of his characters exclaim, 'Hell is other people!' Sometimes it is; more often it is the inner torment projected upon other people. In truth, heaven is other people.

When all else is lost, in war or catastrophe, men and women find each other and discover heaven in the midst of hellish circumstances. When all else is stripped away, other people become infinitely precious. With the loss of all worldly goods and security can come the vision of men and women as persons of infinite value. Heaven, conceived of as a glorious, eternal isolation in ever-expanding blissful consciousness is not heaven at all; it is hell. It is an ego-centred delusion of catastrophic proportions.

Heaven is the Realm of God and of His Holy Angels; of the Mother of God and the Saints, and of men and women in the way of perfection, whose sights are fixed firmly on God and who have come to participation, by Grace, in the Mind of Christ. Heaven is blissful normality. There is an infinity of people to talk to in heaven, and an infinitude of things to talk about, to do, and by the continuing operation of Grace, to become.

Wholeness

A wise and perceptive man once made the assertion that, underlying every religious problem is a sexual problem, and underlying every sexual problem is a religious problem. The two realms, the religious and the sexual, can by no means be separated.

Consecrated virginity is a feature of man's religious expression which is almost world-wide, and this is so when honoured as much in the breach as in the observance. There is something in man which acknowledges the principle of polarity as it exists between Creator and creation, and seeks to respond in a way which is both interiorly and exteriorly faithful to God alone. For some this is a vocation and a sacrifice willingly made. For others, it is imposed upon them by their conditioning or their circumstances, and offered as a sacrifice in order to fulfil a vocation not necessarily connected with it.

Faithfulness to God-given vocations involves sacrifices of all kinds, be that vocation one to parenthood or to the monastic life. Sacrifice is painful on at least one level or it is no sacrifice at all, but it is a mistake to isolate something as fundamental to men and women as their sexuality and suppose that this, and this alone, is the supreme sacrifice short of death. God wills the wholeness of men and women, and wholeness is seldom arrived at by their frozen abstinence from each other in fear of one being polluted by the other. Religious problems, and sexual problems, stem from fear,

133

and fear is morbid by definition, for Perfect Love casteth out fear, as Holy Scripture tells us.

Sexual problems are hedged about by fear, and much of that fear is projected or induced by religious attitudes that persist in regarding sexuality as being in some way unclean, or which blatantly identify sex with sin! This, whenever met with, is clear projection upon others of a torment of guilt within. Where religious and sexual problems are concerned, it is difficult to distinguish the chicken from the egg, and discover which came first!

Sexuality derives from polarity and is the expression of it. Polarity derives in the first instance from the relationship between Creator and creation. Male and female in the created order are, as it were, icons of that ultimate relationship. The inseparability of religion and sexuality follows from that. By the same token the disordering of Man's relationship with God by what we know as the 'Fall from Grace' can hardly have failed to complicate and disorder the whole realm of human sexuality. It is the Original Sin of Man that has overlayed the whole of human sexuality with a deep layer of guilt and which is responsible for its radical disorder. The Adam and Eve myth touches upon this, not without humour, in the episode of the fig leaves. Prior to the Fall there was no guilt, no shame, no awkwardness, no disorder; this is the message of the fig leaves.

It is no surprise, in view of what has been said, that religion is frequently obsessed by sexual considerations. The behaviour of men and women towards each other is a fundamental religious concern. Personal relationships derive from the ultimate Personal relationship of all; that of Creator with creature. Man is one being, and the persons of the being, Man, must behave accordingly. They do not because they are fallen from Grace. Man's loss of integrity is bound up with Man's behaviour: to God, and between men, and between women, and between men and women.

The world maintains an uneasy truce by laws and regulations, backed up by sanctions of vaying degrees of severity.

134

Without these, chaos would be manifest overnight. The world of religion does the same, with more fundamental concerns, but is still, though religious, very much *the world*. The Christian Church, in her disciplines, is adopting the methods of the world; it is difficult to avoid them. But the gospel is the Gospel of Love, and love is the fulfilling of the law and transcends it utterly. Only the Mind of Christ can fulfil human sexuality in faithfulness and truth. And its thoughts are not the world's thoughts, nor are they always those of the worldly Church either.

Healing

Healing is a Ministry of the Church which has been neglected through disbelief. As in the old Israel, prophecy was deemed to end with Ezra, so in the Church, the new Israel, there is a tendency to consign the miraculous to far-off days, to Apostolic times only, or to a mythological dustbin. This is unfaithfulness of a high order and has contributed massively to the sickness of the Church on earth.

Seek, and ye shall find! Expect wholeness and wholeness will be bestowed. Expect miracles and they will happen. Expect, but do not try to define or to find out how and why they happen. Deny the possibility and you cut yourself off from whole dimensions of life. The parameters of a mortal man's mental processes are, in general, far too narrow and criteria of judgement change like the weather.

Healing is a ministry with many dimensions and it is exercised at many different levels, many of them in the purely natural order. All may be good in themselves but in so far as they seek to deal with symptoms only, rather than with underlying causes, they are incomplete. It is the Church's ministry to seek to get to grips with underlying causes; thus Jesus, when confronted with a paralytic, said: 'Thy sins are forgiven thee!'

Sickness is frequently an outward manifestation of an inner disorder at one of a number of levels. But more fundamentally, sickness is an outward manifestation in men and women of the underlying disorder in Man, the being. What happens to man happens to men and women, on earth at any rate, and the very fact of sickness in the human race on earth, and of its many levels and varieties, is an indication of disease in the very being of Man.

Symptoms have to be treated and suffering eased for love's sake, but wholeness comes from a deeper level, transcends sickness and may, on occasion, transfigure it.

Mortal men and women are subject to intense conditioning from the moment of their birth, if not from their very conception. The conditioning is largely subconscious, and guilt, projected, inherited within the whole social ambience and reinforced throughout childhood and adolescence, is the biggest single morbid factor. Guilt is attached to every department of life. Conscious and unconscious taboos hedge every man and woman in on every side and the great majority of their attitudes and judgements are not theirs at all but the product of a massive conditioning.

Conditioning regulates the way in which things are perceived, and indeed what is perceived. Conditioning, to a large degree, determines normal from abnormal, right from wrong. Most moral and value judgements are made in the light of social attitudes, local custom, and the conditioning that goes with them.

This process is inevitable in mortal life but wholeness demands a release from all conditioning and a rediscovery – often a discovery in the first instance – of the realities and of the truth of each individual man and woman. The way of growth into maturity and wholeness is followed by Divine Grace alone. Men and women imagine themselves liberated and free from the attitudes of former generations, but there is no liberation in mere rebellion. Divine Grace is the liberator

136

and it is growth into, and participation in the Mind of Christ which is the state of having been truly liberated and enabled to BE.

The Mind of Christ knows no conditioning. Reality is plain to see. Truth is beyond questioning. The character of things is plain and an overriding Compassion for the self, and in consequence for other selves, characterises all those who partake of this collective, all-conscious Mind.

Wholeness is before all else a state of mind, with the mind abiding where it truly belongs – in the heart.

Men and women must outgrow the whole conditioning process that has contained them since their earliest moments. Rebellion in adolescence is a vital part of this process and though often damaging, it is a natural movement towards the way of perfection. Everything must be capable of being questioned, much will be rejected, temporarily or permanently, but there must be an ambience of love which is sufficient to provide a basic security within which the rebellion can take place. There is a close analogy between the adolescent's questioning within a secure framework of love and the Christian's struggle with doubts and uncertainties within the secure framework of the Faith of the Church as a whole.

The rebellion must be kept alive in principle throughout adulthood. The process of conditioning is unceasing; the world depends upon it. Conditioned attitudes, herd-instincts, group minds of all kinds must be recognized and withdrawn from, for they are slavery. Men and women who seek the way of perfection must sit lightly to the expectations and attitudes of the world in which they are obliged to live, and which they are obliged to serve for love's sake. The tensions involved will often be considerable and there must be no retreat into a cosy, self-righteous isolation. Sometimes the tensions will be destructive in some way or another. Christ was crucified; why should his followers expect favoured treatment?

Christ was crucified by worldly religion. The Church, in so

much as she is an institution, is worldly. It cannot be otherwise. The institution is a worldly phenomenon, and within the institution are other institutions, all with group minds, all heavily conditioned and conditioning. The Christian must learn to sit lightly to institutions as such. The way of maturity leads to the discovery that less and less seems to be important, but that which is important becomes more and more important. A Christian must be able to change his or her mind and be independent of the many group minds and group attitudes that, perforce, impinge upon his or her day to day life and witness in the Faith.

Among the most powerful conditioners of men and women are the churches on earth. The rearing and nurturing of children in the faith involves a conscious conditioning which, in normal circumstances, matures into a conscious, personal faith. Much of the conditioning, conscious and subconscious, has a morbid character, however, as rival church denominations profess exclusive validity or righteousness and condition rising generations into attitudes and judgements which bear little or no relation to truth, and even less to Christian charity or forebearance. In the main, it is the falsehoods and the half-truths which disfigure the presentation of the Faith which cause maturing men and women to fall away, and the more overt manifestations of prejudice and interdenominational hatred are a positive betrayal of the Gospel and a denial of Christ.

Christian men and women must, by the Grace of God, rise above the disfiguring controversies that torment the churches on earth. They must mature until they are bigger by far than the denominational backgrounds from which they came, and by which they came to faith. They must be loyal to their own church, but their first loyalty is to Christ. They must recognize that the unity for which most of them pray already exists, for the unity between the Church on earth and the Church in heaven is unbreakable, and this is the only unity that ultimately matters.

The Church on earth is one in a common Baptism, and one

in her unity with the Church in heaven. The churches are man-made and man-maintained in their disunity. They are upheld in disunion by vested interest and deep conditionings in prejudice and determined mutual ignorance. All men and women are sinners. Divine Grace alone enables a Christian man or woman to rise above denominational conditioning and to maintain integrity, both of their own church and of the Church as a whole. Wholeness demands this of every Christian, and love demands much sacrifice of the lesser good in church concerns if the truth and the reality of Christ in His Church, in heaven and on earth, is to be faithfully proclaimed.

Balance

The Holy Rule of St Benedict provides for a monastic lifestyle that is in as perfect a balance as is attainable in this earthly life. The Rule provides for manual work, study and prayer as a daily occupation. In so doing the total person: body, mind (soul/psyche) and spirit are exercised and kept in harmony within a life dedicated to God. This is the way of wholeness.

Mortal men and women are hard put to it to attain balance in any of these three realms. For some, the body is exalted at the expense of the mind and to the neglect of the spirit. Others neglect the body and exalt the mind. Others neglect both in an unnatural spirituality. Every permutation and combination of error is perpetrated by mortal men and women to the shipwreck of their lives and the frustration of their possibilities.

Balanced diet and proper exercise are fundamental to the health, not only of the body, but of the mind (soul/psyche) and to the spirit. For a man or a woman is a unity. It is necessary to eat in order to pray, as Pierre Teilhard de Chardin reminds us. A proper exercise of the mind by each according to gifts and abilities is equally vital to the health of the body and the spirit. A disciplined interior life, dedicated to God, is essential to the total person and will motivate both mind and body in their own disciplines.

Men and women must do their utmost according to their circumstances and their abilities. It is good that all three levels be stretched and challenged for without this they will not realise their possibilities. Men and women owe God the offering of themselves in wholeness and in as good health and condition as is possible for them in the circumstances in which they are placed.

The disciplines of Hatha-Yoga, allied to creative use of the mind, and meditation leading to contemplation, are a powerful aid to wholeness among city dwellers otherwise deprived of opportunities. But they demand a determination to offer them within the context of a life dedicated to God and leading, by Divine Grace, towards participation in the Mind of Christ.

Men and women must be rooted in the soil before they can grow into their complete selves. The Hebrew word, *Adam*, meaning humanity as opposed to men and women, is derived from a similar word which means 'the dust of the earth'. The burial rite concludes with the words 'ashes to ashes, dust to dust', over the open grave. The Ash Wednesday liturgy contains the words, 'Remember, O Man, that dust thou art and unto dust shalt thou return'. The attempts of some urban men and women to live in separation from the good earth is doomed to failure. Parks, gardens and window-boxes testify to this fundamental need for roots in the soil.

The international organization, the multinational business empire which hops its executives perpetually round the globe from one square office building to another, all over the world, is in danger of denying reality in a singularly hazardous way. A rootless man becomes demonic. Men and women who deny place and culture lose their own humanity. Men and women must have roots and the basic stability that goes with them if they are to become whole, for wholeness is a growth process and does not take place in a state of rootlessness or in a vacuum.

Without the earth and all its creatures, Man must perish, for the earth is his whole *raison d'être* in the first instance. The earth serves man only so long as man serves the earth. Heaven and earth are intertwined, and for a man or a woman to attain to the fullness of heaven it is necessary for their feet to have been set firmly on the ground.

Men and women attain heaven, by Divine Grace, in order to bring the earth with them into heaven. This is their priesthood in the New Covenant. Those who are determined to deny the earth and live in an ever more dehumanising world of their own greedy fantasy have nothing to bring with them; they have denied their fundamental *raison d'être*.

Wholeness

Wholeness is a state of mind. It is also a dynamic state and not static in any way. Most of the ills of mortal men and women have origins which can be described as psychosomatic. Physical symptoms very frequently have mental or emotional causes. There is a collective element in this psychosomatic illness; stress is induced by collective pressures, insecurities in the group minds with which men and women are identified, and projections from other tormented minds, unable to cope with life.

Wholeness proceeds from the heart. A man or a woman who learns to abide with the mind in the heart will begin to rise above more and more of the collective ills and will become silent and still within. Healing at greater and greater depths will become possible and a man or woman in the way of wholeness will be a source of peace and security for others, for peace will surround them.

Wholeness is, in brief, the state which begins to obtain when the mind begins to become accustomed to abiding in the heart. A man or a woman does not seek wholeness only for his or her own health. It is sought for the glory of God and for the benefit of others. Each whole man and woman is a healing for Man, the being. Each fragmented and tormented man or woman is but reflecting the ills of Man as a whole.

There is a sense in which all sickness is psychosomatic in that it is the collective psyche of man which is in disorder, and this collective disorder is manifest in individuals. The healing of Man began when the Word became Flesh and dwelt among us. By the operation of Divine Grace within men and women the healing process, timeless in its origins, continues while time lasts.

Men and women do not attain to wholeness in isolation. They do not attain to heaven in isolation either. The Divine Grace does not work in men and women in isolation from one another. The whole of human life is corporate and men and women become their true selves in ministry to one another within the corporate whole.

The religious problems and sexual problems are intertwined, for both the religious quest and human sexuality are fundamentally concerned with wholeness. Thus men and women have to grow out of the conditionings in which they have grown up and find their own attitudes and make their own judgements.

The quest for wholeness involves a process of healing at every level. It is the healing, in individuals, of the ills of Man, the creature; for Man, the creature, is healed in and through the persons who, together, make up that unity which is Man.

And all this is the work of Divine Grace in men and women, touching, transforming and transfiguring every department of their lives that, in them, the new heaven and the new earth may come into the fullness of their realisation.

Self-Abandonment

Mortal men and women have to learn to let themselves go. The built-in temptation of earthly life is to live as if continued existence depends upon self and the efforts of self. Men and women are acquisitive. Their security is propped up by their circumstances, their possessions, their status – real or imaginary – their carefully constructed images of themselves that they wish to project in order to hide behind. Criteria are as much trivial as they are worldly, and the thought of the whole facade crashing about their ears in ruin is altogether too much for them and has about it all the properties of a nightmare.

Multitudes of men and women live out their lives by criteria of their own or of society's own making and never reach the image with which they have, albeit insecurely, identified. Multitudes die in this condition and their liberation into reality enters a new set of circumstances which are not our present concern. Men and women must learn, by Divine Grace, to come out from behind their brittle fortifications, risk all, and let themselves go.

This takes courage as well as faith. It is only by Divine Grace that it can be attempted. For mortal men and women it is like climbing out of a concrete blockhouse into fresh air. But it is also like climbing into a small boat at night, casting off without oars, engine or rudder, and being swept into a torrent to be carried God only knows where. It is safer to die in the blockhouse than to live in the boat.

To become whole involves letting go. To get to heaven involves letting go, for that is where the raging torrent is flowing. To trust God is to be taken at one's word. The way ahead is an abyss. The leap of faith must be made, in the dark, over and over again in the course of earthly life. The risk is of utter calamity and total loss. To refuse the jump is to disqualify. But as Jesus reminds us, only those who lose their lives will find them. So make the sign of the cross and leap! Make the sign of the cross and cast off the mooring rope! Trust in the Lord and wait for the astonishments!

Self-abandonment to the Divine Providence is by no means to be confused with the adolescent fecklessness of those who resist the duty of growing up and expect others to do their thinking for them and provide for their needs. Self-abandonment is a work of considerable maturity and is possible, by Divine Grace, when a man or a woman has something to abandon! The feckless, the irresponsible, the invincibly immature have nothing until they grow up.

The Prodigal Son was such a one, and he may serve as the beacon of hope for all sinners, but in particular for the steadfastly adolescent. He made his own mistakes, arrived at reality, and at last had something to abandon. He cast himself adrift from his all-devouring ego and returned, not to the father he had grown up with, but the same father who was now his friend.

Self-abandonment is possible only when the ego is recognized for what it is and put firmly in its place. Self-abandonment is a cutting of the ego adrift and, wonder upon wonder, it finds itself by being lost! But it is the ego no more; it has been transfigured.

Self-abandonment is the act of supreme human responsibility and is therefore impossible for the irresponsible. It is an ongoing process rather than a once-for-all act, and requires renewal and rededication throughout earthly life. Self-abandonment is therefore a way of life which is lived by Divine Grace, and in which the things impossible for man are experienced as entirely possible for God.

Self-abandonment is self-sacrifice. It is the acid test of love. It is the gift of the totality of being to the Beloved to do with what he wills. Self-abandonment therefore has its earthly parallels, but the Heavenly Bridegroom is more faithful than His earthly counterpart, and is motivated wholly by the self-abandoning love which was manifest supremely in the Incarnation and upon the Cross.

Holy Poverty

Poverty is identified, in men's minds, with squalor, deprivation and a loss of human dignity. As such it is an ill that should be eradicated. The same word can have a totally different meaning, however, and holy poverty is a state of great Grace.

Holy poverty is not to be identified with outward circumstances for it transcends them. Holy poverty is a state of mind which has let the whole idea of personal possessions go, and which is dependent on God alone without the clutter of so-called belongings complicating life and the Holy obedience to the will of God that is due to God.

Holy poverty is therefore a state of detachment from the things of this world and from all possessions. It is the state of mind which enables a man or a woman to regard the objects surrounding them, which in law might be regarded as possessions, as friends to be looked after at the present time but to be let go at a moment's notice, just as they will have to be let go at the moment of death.

Holy poverty lives with its bags packed and ready for immediate departure. But holy poverty owns no bags nor anything to put in them.

So far from being squalid or deprived, holy poverty is a state of great liberation. So far from being a state in which human dignity is lost or impaired, it is the supreme human dignity on earth, for it is prepared for immediate departure at all times, yet at home wherever it is.

Holy poverty is a state of mind, of soul. It can be attained in a monastic cell by the freely willed embracing of the outward forms of poverty. It can be attained in a king's

palace by detachment from all outward circumstances. It is to be attained by men and women everywhere, for it is the truth of the human condition and its highest mortal expression, but its attainment in any circumstances, be they monastic or imperial, is dependent upon Divine Grace working to transform the human soul from within.

Chastity

Chastity is frequently identified with a total abstinence from intimacies of a physical and overtly sexual nature. This understanding is allied to a fear of sexuality itself, an identification of its formidable powers and pressures with sinfulness and, not infrequently, an attitude of mind which bluntly identifies sex with sin. This is a profoundly morbid and unrealistic attitude which goes a long way towards implicitly denying that the Word became *flesh* and dwelt among us.

Chastity is something quite other than total abstinence. The sexuality of men and women is created by God, expresses the polarity which images the relationship between Creator and creatures, and is itself wholly good and blessed. It is necessary to affirm human sexuality unreservedly and proclaim its blessedness and the joy that belongs to it before chastity can be understood in positive terms at all.

Chastity is essentially the right and proper use and expression of human sexuality. It acknowledges sexuality as God-given and blessed. It is sensitive to the subtleties of human relationships, each one of which is unique. It is realistic about the powers and pressures involved and it seeks to exercise a living and compassionate restraint.

Chastity knows no inhibitions but practices discipline and restraint. Chastity behaves in a manner consistent with the relationships within which it is exercised and is careful to give expression to truth at all times. In some circumstances,

146

and for the fulfilment of some vocations, chastity involves a total restraint and the sacrifices that attend it.

For fallen, sinful men and women, chastity is impossible. But by Divine Grace all things are possible, and the man or woman who begins to participate in the Mind of Christ finds that the body begins to be motivated by the spirit and to give more and more truthful expression, both in action and restraint, to the promptings of Divine Love in and through human relationships.

Chastity is a virtue which is not arrived at in a day. It is a triumph of Divine Grace in sinful men and women, a wonder to them, and their joy.

Obedience

The way of obedience leads directly to participation in the Mind of Christ. The way of obedience is followed only by Divine Grace. It is a supreme discipline of the will which learns to transcend feelings, preferences and outward circumstances, and cling to the will of God as that will is revealed.

There is an outward obedience which nurtures the inner obedience in the stages of immaturity. Monastic obedience and military discipline differ in style but have much in common. The will learns to obey, to defer to others, to undertake hardships of all kinds until a growth in inner maturity enables the mind to understand and appreciate the reasons for such curious outward impositions. The ego learns its place and a higher authority determines what the priorities are and what may or may not be done.

This is a childhood all over again, but on a higher plane. Most men and women serve neither in the armed forces nor in the cloister. The disciplines of both are the necessary disciplines of maturity writ large and directed to a specific end. In ordinary life the virtue of obedience, the inner obedience which is the end-product of outward discipline, is arrived at in different ways.

Obedience and responsibility are two sides of the same coin. By the same token disobedience and irresponsibility go together and partake of the nature of sin. Obedience and responsibility are impossible for fallen man. Only by the Divine Grace can they manifest in mortal men and women, and only then can the Priesthood of Man be faithfully exercised.

The three virtues: poverty, chastity and obedience are the hallmarks of mature humanity, but the maturity is that of grace and not of unaided nature, for the Fall of Man has fixated man on the lesser good. He worships an ego-godhead and only by the crucifixion of the will can its resurrection by Divine Grace be effected. Poverty, chastity and obedience are the supreme fruits of self-abandonment to the Divine Providence.

Self-abandonment involves the recognition of realities. The first to be recognized is self-evident, but easy to miss. It is that mortal men and women have but one point of contact with Almighty God, and that is the present moment. Yesterday is dead, tomorrow is not yet born. Only today exists. Having done great things for God in time past is of no consequence. Intending to do great things for God next week is of no value. The only thing that matters is seeking to do the Will of God today, and more important still, this very moment. Only the present moment exists for mortal men and women.

The Hebrew language has two tenses: the past and the future. Strictly speaking there is no present tense as it is understood in most European languages. The present is therefore 'on the move' all the time. The present is being passed through in the journey from the past into the future. The present moment does not exist.

Only the present moment exists; the present moment does not exist. These two ideas must be held together for both are statements of truth. The present moment is not static but dynamic; it gives place to the next, and the next, and the next. The past recedes, the future advances to meet us, and we are at present in a dynamic NOW.

All time is present to Almighty God. All is a 'perpetual now' and nothing is lost. But for mortal men and women, though it is by the whole tenor of their lives that they will be judged, the present moment is of supreme consequence, for *that* is the moment of truth. Only NOW is real and immediate. It is only NOW that is the context for the operation of the human will.

To dwell upon the past is to lose hold on reality. To speculate about the future is to lose hold on reality. Forward planning is a present duty, but it is the exercise of the will NOW, 'while it is called today', that is the work which is enabled by Divine Grace and which is the faithful exercise of the Priesthood of Man.

Man is created to be responsible. Responsibility at any level has to be learned for it is associated with maturity. Wilful refusal to grow up is, by its nature, sinful for it is a denial of humanity, a refusal of *raison d'être*.

The disciplines by which a man or a woman matures into full responsibility by Divine Grace are accepted in love and for love's sake; for as Jesus declared: 'he that loves me will do as I say'.

The Church on earth is that body of men and women who seek, for love's sake, to do what Jesus Christ says. Their failures are incessant, tragic and scandalous, but they are all sinners. The disciplines of the Holy Church are accepted by sinners for Love's sake. They are a part of the growth in Grace by which men and women enter into the Mind of Christ and become the people God created them to be.

In the final analysis however, a man or a woman must stand up and look the Lord in the eyes. Every man must answer for himself. Every woman bears her own responsibility. Nobody can ultimately plead that their sins, their loss of integrity, is the fault of somebody else.

149

Maturity answers for itself. Maturity acknowledges its faults and life's failures, and the list may be a long one and the failures grievous. Maturity is able to be honest and cast itself upon the Divine Mercy because it holds nothing back and faces truth without pretence or excuses. Maturity, however irresponsible it has been in the course of its growth in grace, is ultimately able to accept responsibility and to exercise it.

Maturity in a man or a woman is the state of having abandoned self to the Divine Providence. It is Life Eternal.

Penitence

Penitence lies at the heart of all joy. Penitence and thanksgiving are two sides of the same coin and without them no man or woman attains to the fullness of humanity.

The ego, when left to its own devices, will have nothing to do with penitence for it is a god and everything must fall down before it. The ego will acknowledge no fault for it is faultless and all must conform to it. By the same token the ego will never give thanks, for all things are its right and there is nothing to give thanks for. The ego will take and consume without ceasing, for is it not a god?

Men and women must be liberated from domination by the ego. There is a liberation in the natural order through the disciplines of childhood and the rough encounters with other egos in which most of them become dislodged. But the real liberation is a work of Divine Grace which opens up the perception to criteria so utterly transcendent, so absolute, that penitence must ensue. Penitence is painful to begin with. Disciplines of self-examination and sacramental confession and absolution train the soul into the way of penitence. But the more deeply the soul *becomes* penitent the more deeply it also *becomes* thanksgiving as the limitless extent of the Divine Love is revealed.

150

In a manner of speaking, the process then turns inside out as the soul makes the blessed discovery that he or she is a sinner, accepted as a sinner, loved as a sinner with an Everlasting Love, and ascended into heaven as a sinner in the resurrected and ascended humanity of Christ.

Penitence then becomes a joy, and thanksgiving becomes a way of life. The Church's life is Eucharistic. Eucharist means 'thanksgiving'. At the altar the soul enters into, and is perpetually renewed in, the way of everlasting penitence and thanksgiving which is the life of those who know themselves sinners forgiven, redeemed, and loved with an Everlasting Love.

Intercession

Intercession is the whole life of a priest. Man is God's priest to the earth which he inhabits and the world of half-truths and false criteria is the measure of his spoiled priesthood.

Men and women, all persons of the one being, express their love for one another in intercession. Intercession is a gift of the self to God and an identification of the self with God's Love for the other. Christians, who participate in the High Priesthood of Christ, plead the sacrifice of Christ – the supreme act of Divine Love – in intercession for their fellowmen. In the self-offering of Christ the self-offering of the Christian is caught up and he or she becomes a channel of Divine Grace by virtue of that self-offering.

Men and women must *become* intercession. Intercession stems always from the heart, and no activity will more surely root the mind in the heart than the self-forgetting union of hearts between a man or a woman in prayer and the great Lover of souls. Unless men and women lose themselves they cannot be found. To be lost in self-forgetting intercession is to be found, for love is identified with Love and Divine Grace is released, both in the intercessor and in the one for whom

151

intercession is made, for we are members one of another.

The Eucharist is the supreme intercessory prayer of the Church, and in its context Christian men and women can offer their most profound intercessions. The whole life of the Church is intercessory. Intercession is what she is for. The Great High Priest pleads at her every altar and is both celebrant and victim at every Eucharist.

It is at the altar that Christians, met together, become the Church. It is the great act of corporate self-abandonment in which she is lost in intercession in order that all mankind may be ultimately found.

Death

The ultimate self-abandonment is that of death. But death, the final loss, is the ultimate finding of the true self in the Beloved. Death is the consummation of the union between Christ, the Heavenly Bridegroom and the Church, His Bride. And what is true for the many is true for the one.

The death of Christ on the cross was His consummation of the union of God and man which was His ministry, and which was the truth of His own being. Death was the final and absolute act of self-abandonment of God in Christ to Man. Death, released and transformed, is the ultimate act of self-abandonment of men and women to God.

The consummation of every earthly marriage is a death of both parties and a resurrection to a new and wholly other life of union. This images the consummation of the union of Christ with a Christian. Death is the ultimate act on earth of Holy Communion.

And so death and adoration are two sides of a coin. Men and women must *become* adoration. Adoration is the total loss of self in love for the beloved, an everlasting ecstasy of Love, Peace and Joy.

The name and value of that coin is Life Eternal.